# JULIA CARLSON

# LET'S GET YOU FIRED

How Entrepreneurs Scale to 8 Figures by Letting Go and Leading with Vision

# LET'S GET YOU FIRED

How Entrepreneurs Scale to 8 Figures by
Letting Go and Leading with Vision

To request permissions, contact the publisher at publish@joapublishing.com

Hardcover ISBN: 978-1-967575-52-7
Paperback ISBN: 978-1-967575-51-0
eBook ISBN: 978-1-967575-53-4
Printed in the USA.

Joan of Arc Publishing
Meridian, ID 83646
www.joapublishing.com

# DEDICATION

For my peers, the Visionary Founders,

may your ideas rise, your impact ripple,

and your work transform every life it touches.

# TABLE OF CONTENTS

# INTRODUCTION

# BEFORE AND AFTER

**M**y smile muscles were exhausted after an incredible afternoon spent on the Willamette River in Oregon wine country aboard The Willamette Queen, a famous steamboat, with 40 of my clients. It had been a perfect day, laughing, celebrating and connecting with my client base, and I was feeling that unique sense of accomplishment that only comes from my career: I made it. I DID it. I was successful. But more than that, I had built a team of three, our revenue had surpassed $500,000, I had cultivated wonderful clients, and the good fortune and insight to show appreciation and gratitude to them for doing business with me and my team. And then, everything in my world changed in an instant.

There are moments in our lives that serve as lines of demarcation. The days are known as before, and the days to come will be the after. I just didn't know that *that* day, the priceless sunny Oregon summer day was to be one of those days.

When I finally stepped off the massive steamboat feeling both grateful for my clients and elation at all the hard work which had brought me to this point, I looked to see that my phone was a mess of messages with texts in ALL CAPS and numerous missed calls. I felt the panic and fear set in, and my vision seemed to slow and yet move quickly at the same time. That bitter bite of knowing something was very wrong but not having all the data to process was a certain hell of what felt like a lifetime, but was actually a few minutes. I finally reached my husband's best friend, Joe, who delivered the sentence no mother ever wants to hear: my parents and oldest daughter had been in a head-on collision with a drunk driver. My daughter, Katelyn, was being life-flighted to Randall Children's Hospital. No one could tell me if she was alive.

I dropped to the ground and screamed into the phone, "IS MY DAUGHTER ALIVE?"

No answer. He didn't know. My parents were in the ER. Katelyn was en route via helicopter.

After the moment of not knowing if I would ever see my daughter alive again, the only memories I can grasp of that time were ones of chaos. Chaos in my thinking, feeling, and breathing, which made everything appear warped and discolored like my vision was blurred. It left the outlines of objects and people's faces soft and fuzzy as my assistant drove me to the hospital. In perfect synchronicity, I arrived as the helicopter was landing, and I gripped the hot chain-linked fence with my cold hands watching as they brought her out on a stretcher with my husband closely following the emergency team.

At that time, I had three children under the age of nine and a marriage strained by the demands of raising them with two entrepreneur parents. I was hell-bent on building a thriving business, reinvesting every dollar back into it instead of taking much home, while we relied heavily on my husband's income. I was hustling to grow and scale my financial services firm, often working twelve-hour days, occasionally more. Some days, I would commute four hours to meet with clients in a different branch, make house calls to people I'd never met, and catch up on extra work during the weekends. Did I mention that I was also a competitive bodybuilder at the time? Lifting weights with a trainer during my lunch break? Some people called me driven. Others called me crazy. I think I was a little of both.

The relentless drive and force I led the company with was not sustainable from Katelyn's bedside. While I was unaware of it at the time, looking back, her accident was the tough spark of a new chapter in my life that led me to build the business and life of my dreams.

I had been in hustle mode in my business to build, Build, BUILD! I only knew how to work harder and longer and didn't know another way. The never-ceasing internal voice of "Do more, Do More, MORE!" I had been using as a framework for my life was, in an instant, irrevocably shattered and in that moment, I had to restructure every aspect of my life. That change didn't happen overnight (even though, sometimes, I wish it did), but it started in that hospital room and continued over a series of years in which planned exits, strategic actions, and bold moves were implemented. In short, I had to find it within me to completely trust myself enough to surrender to what I had already created and what I would continue to build: a solid team, business, and expansive empire that needed to no longer function with me as its main employee. In fact, I was actually holding the business back by my choices to be in all places, in all ways, for all things.

*You want a marketing strategy? Great, I'll schedule you at 8pm tonight to go over some details.*

*Oh, there's a new client? Yes, I can take them tomorrow during my lunch break.*

*A last-minute emergency from a new client needing to make a retirement contribution by the April 15th deadline? No problem, I would drop everything, and offer to come pick up the check at their home. In the middle of nowhere. Just me.*

I went out of my way all the time to accommodate and win business with a strategy I was forced to discover did not serve me, my clients, or the purpose and vision of the business I was building. I would make *their emergency my urgency* and that style of management created a weather system that flooded my personal life with havoc. My actions prioritized my business over everything else in life, including my family, and I didn't know how to get out of it or change. And as they say, necessity is the mother of invention. This accident was the unfortunate catalyst for me to realize that I couldn't keep going. I had to figure out how to be a better business owner, how to get out of my own way, and what was more terrifying than that reckoning was: *I had no idea how to do it.*

Nothing about the way I got here was pretty. I crawled; a slow, painful crawl. At 19, I went to work as a teller in a bank, and by 23, I went out on my own with no pedigree or fancy letters after my name. Sure, I could have stayed there for another 10 more years to work my way up to Financial Advisor, but instead, I built my first 7 figures while trying to outrun how small and unseen I felt at home, and to make sure I could support my family if I was ever left alone. Instead of facing my difficult marriage, I buried myself in twelve-hour days and the sweet hit of being needed. Clients came first. I was focused. I measured my worth in full calendars and commissions and I numbed the ache with late-night shopping bags I hid in the trunk.

Then the call came: the head-on collision. The ICU. Hearing my voice ask, "Is my daughter alive?" That was the moment that led to me wondering, weeks later, if my company would collapse if I chose her bedside instead of my business. While my team was absolutely trustworthy, I didn't know how to trust them. Truthfully, I'd trained them to depend on me. I sat next to Katelyn's ICU bed triaging emails, bargaining with God and my inbox, and then, I chose my kid. Shockingly, the company didn't die; my illusion of control did. What I had was a stubborn sense of self worth that was tied to accomplishment. That season, and the surrender it forced, is why I could build an 8-figure business the long, unglamorous way. I'm here because I owned the mess, fired myself, rebuilt with values and structure, and learned to lead without abandoning the people I love, including me.

If you have scaled your business to a major six-figure level (think $500K+), I know your life and business probably feel really, really hard right now. I know there are days when your workload feels overwhelming; you're drowning in your inbox, to-do list, team and client meetings, important initiatives that keep getting pushed aside, and the constant pressure of payroll. Heavy is the head that wears the crown, because at this stage of building your empire, all of your people depend on you and you *alone* to provide them their salaries. I know that, and I've been there. I relate to feeling an entrepreneur's ambition and their drive to grow and scale something massive and impactful. I feel their passion for their creation, and their exhaustion. And I can sense the strain in their relationships with their partner, or kids, or the lack of desire and time to find a partner. All of this can lead to loneliness, causing you to feel misunderstood and misaligned by those closest to you wondering, *Why don't they get this?* Or maybe you experience

5

support from your loved ones and community, but with the weight of the world on your shoulders, it doesn't seem to make a difference.

Maybe you carry guilt because you have become "*that parent,*" the one who never volunteers for the field trip. And that email about the family barbeque and how they want you to bring your famous cheesecake? Yeah, you intentionally ignored that email because, truthfully, you're tapped out. Or that lunch date with your friend? Yes, you had to cancel again.

Or, worse, when your daughter says to you while clinging tightly to her favorite Snuggie with a swipe of spaghetti sauce on her cheek, "Mom, I want to be a client, so I can spend time with you."

*Ouch.*

And, yes, that happened with Jasmine, my middle child.

You made the sacrifices: long nights, missed dates with your partner, and the quiet drain of 12-hour days. You didn't pay yourself because you chose to reinvest in your dream. The business you built, the one you love, also brings you stress, pressure, and loneliness. Most days it costs you peace, connection, and maybe even your joy. And, you look around towards all the corners of your life thinking, *Is this all there is?*

It's a fair question to ponder now that you have launched, grown and passed the startup phase. You're doing or approaching 7 figures in revenue. That's *elite*. You're already in the top 4% of all businesses, and for women-owned companies, fewer than 2% ever get here. You've achieved what most entrepreneurs never will—and that needs to be said out loud. Out of 33 million small businesses in the U.S., only a tiny fraction cross the $1 million mark, and you're one of them.

(Source: U.S. Census Bureau, SBA, American Express State of Women-Owned Business Report.)

The next level, the leap to eight figures, is rarer still. Public-facing data suggest that less than 1% of U.S. companies ever generate $10 million or more in annual revenue. Many stall in that stretch between $1 and $10 million, what's often called the valley of death. Not because they stop working hard, but because effort alone can't take you there.

That leap requires something different. A reinvention of identity, systems, team, leadership, and value architecture: the inner and outer evolution that my Entrepreneurial Spiral™ and Fire Yourself Framework™ were designed to guide.

What you've built is already extraordinary. That's just who YOU are.

But even powerhouses get tired. Even visionaries hit the point where the hustle feels heavier than it used to. You're still running the show, still grinding, still carrying the weight of it all. Still feeling like you are the business. You know there's more growth ahead, more impact you want to make, more freedom to expand into, yet the path feels like it demands more of you than you have left to give.

You're still *doing it all.*

So you take a sip of your second coffee, hoping for clarity, and the whispers comes:

- "I can't keep going like this."
- "No one can do it like me."
- "I have to be the one."
- "I miss out too much with my kids."
- "My partner doesn't understand."
- "Being busy makes me feel good."
- "Making money makes me feel successful."
- "I want to prove something to myself and the world."

I know these words because they were *my* words.

I lived this. I *am* you. And I'm here to tell you, there is another way. The way I learned was because of an accident on Oregon Route 34. What if the answer isn't what you think it is? What if the next level isn't more hustle, but less? What if you don't have to do it all? What if there's a new path to freedom, one built on trust, surrender, and strategy?

As humans, we are messy, complex creatures and even on our best days, walking contradictions. Some days, we will have vastly different sides of our big brains or hearts that come screaming into the world. We can push, prove, and burn ourselves out only then wonder, where is the break, the softness, the flow we long for in our lives? We experience deep, often profound, emotions that can make us do more, drive more, and in the end, will deplete us. In business, we often over-rely on our "doing more" part of ourselves. I know because I've lived the hard way. And I found a better one.

You don't have to choose between your dream and your personal life, partner, or children. You don't have to choose between impact and intimacy.

But first, you must stop trying to do it alone.

That change begins with a shift in mindset, or what I call, **breaking the mental glass ceiling.**

Since you're reading this, you have self-selected into the group of entrepreneurs that have slayed revenue dragons, survived market chaos, and led a team (including yourself) with courage. *You've built an empire.* Now, it's time to stop overexerting yourself, proving your worth, and let go of your starring role in your business so you can be the starring role of your legacy.

The strategies that get you to 7 figures are not the ones that will take you to 8 and beyond. What worked to get you here won't work to get you *there*. And, there? Oh, that's the sweet spot. That's you actually living out what is on your vision board!

In fact, to scale to the next level, you'll have to do something bold. Something that sounds counterintuitive. ***You'll have to fire yourself.***

And as a founder, that can feel rather uncomfortable.

Let's be clear: this isn't about giving up your power or stepping back. It's about stepping into a new kind of power. Not the hustle-fueled, white-knuckle power you had to draw upon to build your business to where it is today. Don't get me wrong, there is a time and place for this kind of push. But now, you need to develop a deeper, freer, more expansive power; the kind that creates lasting wealth, impact, and joy for you.

In my experience, there are two frameworks required to build a truly successful business. One is internal, one external. They are the yin and yang of sustainable success. The Entrepreneurial Spiral™ is the internal process, the evolution of who you are as a founder, while the Fire Yourself Framework™ is the external structure that supports how your business grows and scales. They work in harmony. When you experience rapid external growth, the internal side calls for expansion. And when you make an internal breakthrough, whoosh—the external will often catch up. Each fuels the other. Both are essential.

This book is your guide to the process of firing yourself so you can rise higher and create the legacy and impact your heart truly desires. You're not just firing yourself from tasks and roles, but from the mindset that says you have to do it all. From the guilt and shame around money and success. From the belief that success has to be hard, lonely, and exhausting.

There is a better way. I promise.

# CHAPTER 1

# THE ENTREPRENEURIAL SPIRAL™ THE PATH OF BECOMING

I used to run—a lot—to keep from burning out. I'd lace up my shoes and pop a self-improvement disc into my CD Walkman. Those tapes and CDs were the forerunner to podcasts, and I would listen to Tony Robbins or anything that kept my mind sharp, as I headed into the rugged hills behind my home in rural Oregon. I wasn't running for fun. I was running because the pressure in my business and personal life had nowhere else to go. I was running because I didn't know how to slow down without feeling like I was falling apart.

It was always the same hills. The same steep climbs with blind curves. The same winding roads through the spruce forest where we've lived for nearly 30 years. I know every bend, every grade. It became a personal ritual in a way that only an outdoor gym can symbolize. And the more I ran the exact same trails, the more I noticed something weird. I was also facing the same paths in my professional life; money stress, team chaos, self-doubt. I'd solve the issues, feel on top of the world... and then, they would show up again, months later. Same pattern, but in a new disguise.

At first, it made me feel like I was doing something wrong, like I'd missed a step going up a flight of stairs. I would get frustrated and sometimes bored with the repetition.

But one day, somewhere between mile three and mile four, it hit me: my body was tired, but not in the usual way. It wasn't burnout. It was something else, something deeper. Something was surfacing. And as my feet hit the pavement in my comfortable rhythm, I understood: I wasn't just repeating the same challenges, I was rising *through* them.

I had been here before, but I wasn't the same.

I wasn't stuck in a cycle. I was growing through one. The same challenges resurfaced, but I would respond from a higher place.

This wasn't failure on repeat; this was something completely different.

I had been building something all along; a business, a life, a self, and it was unfolding in a pattern I hadn't yet seen clearly. It wasn't linear, like a ladder. It wasn't a straight line. It was something else entirely: a moving, living, ever-changing experience. *A spiral.*

The spiral wasn't a concept I read in a book or picked up at a mastermind. It was something I felt deep inside myself; a unique experience that was both somatic and revelatory.

Each time the challenge returned, I met it with a little more clarity, a little more wisdom, and a little more power. Like I finally figured out how to use the focus on a fancy camera and, suddenly, everything snapped into clarity. It was the "ah-ha!" moment I so desperately chased on those pine tree trails. What once broke me now barely fazes me. What once derailed me now deepens my resilience.

I call it the Entrepreneurial Spiral™, and it's how I've shattered every mental glass ceiling I've ever faced.

The spiral isn't just a theory. It's rhythm. It's how transformation really happens. You don't ascend in straight lines. You circle back. You revisit. You meet yourself again at new heights. Not because you failed, but because you're still growing. That's the pattern fueling the invisible, internal change inside you.

This is the inner work of a successful CEO, founder, or any business owner. The key is building trust within yourself because the biggest lie most people believe is that the answers are *out there.* When the truth is, the answer is IN YOU. This "out there" thinking often sounds like: If I only do this, or hire this person, or bring a new coach on board. While all of these actions can be powerful, they can also feed into your belief that you lack something you already have. That's chaos and it's a common experience most entrepreneurs have. Add to it the fact that growth doesn't happen in a straight line and you're in a full-blown crisis. It's the very pattern you see reflected in the failure rate of most businesses.

Here's what I've unlocked and taught my team, my clients, and now you: imagine climbing a mountain where the only way up is a spiral path. The rock face is too steep for a direct ascent, so you loop. Again and again. You hit the same fog you've seen before, but now you know it won't last. You hear the same voice of doubt, but this time, you don't believe it. You're not on the same loop; you're elevating higher.

Most people believe the terrain is what takes them out. But it's not. It's what they can't see. The spiral doesn't stall because of what's ahead of you. It stalls because of what's still unresolved inside of you.

That's where mental ceilings live. And those are the ones we're here to shatter.

There comes a moment on every entrepreneur's journey when things stop working, not because the systems broke or the market shifted, but because something unseen gets triggered. You're still moving, just not forward. You're still pushing, but nothing is breaking through. Something inside you hits a wall.

It's not the economy.
It's not your team.
It's not your offer.
It's *you*.

These are the thresholds no one sees, but the entrepreneur feels. The beliefs and old identities that sneak in when you're tired, successful, or on the verge of something bigger. You think you're stuck because you've made a mistake. But what's really happening is that your current mindset has taken you as far as it can. To rise again, something must break.

That's the mental glass ceiling.

It isn't loud or obvious, and it won't ping your calendar. Usually, you don't realize you've hit it until you're banging your head against it, then the message lands: *This is as far as you go. You're not ready for the next level.*

When you're caught in linear thinking, every repeated challenge feels like failure. You find yourself saying things like, *"I already dealt with this, why is it happening again?"* It feels like you're back at the bottom of the mountain, like all your progress has vanished.

But that's the lie.

Spiral thinking reveals something else entirely. It says: *"I've been here before, but I'm not the same person I was last time."* This isn't repetition. It's a return with greater awareness. You're meeting the same themes whether money, leadership, visibility, or fear, but from a higher level of self.

You're not starting over. You're evolving. And climbing ever higher as you go; every spiral brings one. That's how you know you're growing.

The Entrepreneurial Spiral™ doesn't promise that you'll never face the same challenge twice; it promises that each time, you'll be better equipped to lead through it, and hopefully, rise faster. Breaking a mental ceiling isn't a business tactic; it's your becoming as an entrepreneur. If you allow it, it can be one of the most meaningful experiences of your life.

I became elegant on my own entrepreneurial path. And who you become on your journey will be unique because the spiral will push you to become the best version of yourself, whatever that may mean to you. This is where business isn't about business; it's about the version of you that you want to be. And if that is a spiritually aligned business owner, fantastic! If that is a work two hours a day owner, wonderful! This isn't just business, it's the art of being. Everything you could ever want to learn about yourself or evolve into can be learned through building a business. Once you grasp that, it's so much easier and a lot more fun.

If you expect your path to be linear, detours feel like failure. See the spiral, and you'll recognize the pattern of becoming.

Each cycle strips away what no longer fits: outdated mindsets, old survival patterns, and inherited beliefs that were never chosen. What's left behind isn't just clarity, it's freedom; a way of being that's no longer driven by fear, proving, or performance. It's a grounded sense of truth that allows you to move through life with integrity, alignment, and ease.

This is the deeper work of your unshakeable identity that is grounded in wholeness, self-trust, and true freedom. Those are the real rewards. The path isn't just about building a business that lasts; it's about becoming someone who no longer needs to strive for worth. Someone who operates from a place of truth, not tension.

Our wholeness as entrepreneurs isn't perfection or balance. It's coherence. It's when the inner world matches the outer one that self-trust takes a seat at the table: thoughts, decisions, and actions reflecting a self that no longer buys into fear, but from presence and aligned purpose—the hallmarks of personal freedom.

For years, I thought building my business would give me freedom, but the truth is, the business was never the destination, it was just the vehicle. The Entrepreneurial Spiral™ revealed the map that led me to wholeness—the ultimate internal result.

It's the invisible ceilings we hit, the mental limits, the stories we've outgrown, the beliefs that kept us safe at one level, but now keep us stuck, that create friction. And that's where the real work lives; it's the juice that's worth the squeeze.

You grow into the entrepreneur you're meant to be by moving through a five-stage rhythm in the spiral, not in a neat sequence, and not just once. Those same five stages drive every breakthrough I've experienced, and every transformation I've led for my clients. The rhythm holds. The rise is inevitable.

Progress.

Plateau.

Reflection.

Reinvention.

Rise.

Repeat.

## Progress

Begin where the momentum is made—*Progress*. All progress starts with action. And from those actions, confidence follows. I know that seems counterintuitive, but it's true.

But not all action is equal. Movement that comes through what I call inspired action; action guided by intuition or by whatever internal compass you trust most, is what drives the progress you deeply desire. For me, my inspired action stems from a knowing and a deep connection to God. I get insights and nudges that lead me to my best actions: send this letter, open this branch, say 'no' to the event. Each decision ultimately guides me toward my best self.

As entrepreneurs, when those marching orders come through our internal guidance system, our job is to act. NOW. Delaying only allows the usual suspects of shame, guilt, regret, or fear to simmer inside us. Once that emotional downward spiral begins, taking action can become difficult, even impossible.

But inspired action will *always break* that cycle.

This type of action is fueled by the four D's. It starts with Desire, clearly recognizing what you want and allowing yourself to embrace it. Desire then leads to Decision, the point where you eliminate all other options and commit. This decision energizes Determination, the resolve to keep going when the going gets tough. Finally, determination builds Discipline; the daily choices that align your life with your vision.

Discipline is not restriction. And it's certainly not deprivation. It is the container that holds your freedom. Waking early to run, saying no to things you might really love (TV, staying out late, releasing caffeine) for something bigger, like focusing your energy on a new offer. These are the acts that protect and enable the life you want. The structure you build is what allows you to move with greater ease, to decide without doubt, and to live without constant negotiation.

Inspired action isn't always pretty, but it is always progress. It's the self-guided decision to move, not because everything is ready, but because you are. It's the release of permission, the internal "yes" that comes before the external proof, the birthplace of confidence. You first step into being, then you do, and then you have the confidence.

Confidence is born when you act from your inspired future self. That's the first step of the spiral. Progress.

## Plateau

Plateaus aren't always a bad thing. They can be incredibly frustrating, but they are a crucial period for building your foundation. The experience can be uncomfortable, but the mindset you need is curiosity. This is the space where you ask deeper questions, where you analyze the constraints. What was working before, and why isn't it working now?

Maybe this is a good time to restructure your team, add a new member, or release someone whose growth has stalled. The person who helped you reach this plateau may not want to go further with you. And that's okay.

Your mind might scramble for control: do more, push harder, find the fix. But what's needed here isn't force; that will break the playfulness that curiosity requires. What you do need is presence with your frustration. It's totally uncomfortable because the old tools, the ones you loved so much, stop working.

The ceiling in this stage can be quiet and might feel like a moving target. It might tell you you're falling behind because things have slowed and convince you that momentum is the only metric that matters.

But seeking deeper insight into how you are showing up, creating and building this business will push you to the next stage. In a plateau, if you let curiosity lead, you turn frustration into growth.

## Reflection

Reflection requires time. Time to be intentional, to sit with the realities of your life, and see a bigger field with greater clarity. It's the pause that helps you notice what is no longer working and the lessons hidden within that understanding. The curiosity you cultivated during the plateau now opens the door to the insights you need at this moment.

It may seem like you don't have time to reflect, but that is exactly when you need it. This is where the deepest learning happens. You start to integrate what you're understanding, while accepting both the reality that brought you here and the truth that change is necessary to reach the next level.

Reflection requires your honesty. It is the willingness to examine what you've created and recognize what no longer aligns.

The ceiling here is avoidance. It encourages you to stay busy, helpful, and moving—anything to avoid stopping long enough to feel what needs to be felt. But reflection requires that you stop, listen, and allow what is true to grow.

## Reinvention

Reinvention begins the moment you stop clinging to who you once were. It takes courage to move forward in a different way. What once felt undeniably true may no longer fit because you are no longer the same person. It might have been true for the version of you who hadn't yet gained new knowledge, sat in the plateau, or taken the time to reflect. Reflection teaches you the lessons; reinvention is the opportunity to apply those lessons, to change, and to choose differently.

Courage will be your best friend in Reinvention, and letting go will shape your mindset.

Reinvention is the commitment to choose another way. It is the quiet release of what no longer serves you, the deliberate decision to stop defaulting. It is the choice to stop saying yes to what no longer resonates, to stop proving, chasing, or pretending.

This isn't always something that happens with a flashy rebrand or with rapid social media posts. That may be part of your strategy in reinventing yourself to become more visible, but it doesn't *have* to be. It can look like small, deliberate choices, repeated until they become who you are. The courage needed here doesn't have to be loud or showy; it just needs to be steady.

Because that's the only thing that will allow an old identity to fall away without rushing to fill the space with validation, pushing or proving. It trusts that the space itself is part of becoming.

## Rise

Rise isn't the result of the spiral. It's the reward of your mental rewiring.

You don't rise because you pushed through. You rise because you Surrendered what was no longer aligned with who you were becoming. You shed the story. You rewrote the rule. You trusted the pause. You chose to become the one who could hold more without losing yourself.

The mindset here isn't about triumph. It's about integration. It's about wholeness. A steadiness that can't be shaken by outcomes.

Rise is the quiet power of coherence. Your thoughts, actions, and presence all moving in the same direction. For me, sometimes, it didn't feel like I was climbing, it just felt like simply being. It becomes second nature, and the rhythm feels normal, like a heartbeat encouraging me.

That's the gift of the spiral: it doesn't rush. It reveals itself and maintains a steady pace. And when you meet it with the right mindset, you don't just grow. You become.

## The 30,000 Foot View

I can teach you the systems and give you the exact blueprint to scale your business to 8 figures and beyond. I've done it, I've helped others do it, across different industries. But if you don't get this, if you don't understand the Entrepreneurial Spiral™, the identity shifts, and the inner glass ceilings, you'll sabotage every strategy I give you.

Because no system can outperform your mindset. No structure can hold what your self-concept is unwilling to accept.

Building an 8-figure business isn't just about scaling and growth. It's about becoming the version of you who can handle that level of expansion without collapsing under the weight of old programming.

This is what the spiral teaches you: how to grow and, then, how to hold and receive what you've grown into.

When an entrepreneur hits a plateau and the spiral tightens, the pressure builds in places you can't always identify. You crave simplicity. You miss the days when it was just you and your laptop. You fantasize about quitting, going small, and making everything quiet again.

But you can't go back.

The version of you that started this journey no longer exists. Shrinking now would feel like self-abandonment.

The only way forward is up. And up doesn't mean harder. It means higher. It means lighter. It means alignment.

I've experienced this spiral more times than I can count. What I've realized is that every breakdown along the way was really a breakthrough in disguise. The spiral doesn't just bring you back to the same problems. It shows you how to see them differently. It sharpens you. It breaks you open. It reintroduces you to the truth of who you are and who you are becoming, layer by layer.

When I left the bank at 23 to start my wealth management firm, I wasn't just making a career move. I was breaking a glass ceiling within myself. I had the licenses. I had the experience. But I had no seat at the table. And I knew if I waited for permission, I'd have to wait a decade. So I leapt. I started my own business and launched myself into the spiral.

During the 2008 recession, the business I had built buckled under the weight of a crashing market while I was pregnant with my third child. Clients panicked. The systems we depended on failed. That was a plateau season, and it required reinvention. It took three years, a fresh start with a new broker-dealer, and a deep willingness to evolve. But I did it. And the downward spiral lifted again.

In 2012, the accident changed everything. My grip on control, my Hustle, my identity as the one who had to hold it all; that illusion shattered. That moment cracked me open. And it became the start of true Surrender. It didn't feel like growth. It felt like grief. But it marked the rise of a different kind of power.

Even writing this book pulled me into a ceiling. The thoughts came quickly: *Who am I to lead this? Who am I to challenge entrepreneurs to grow, scale, and give?* I could stay in my comfort zone. I could hide inside my success. But I knew that wasn't the way. The spiral was moving again. And my next level was calling.

There have been quieter ceilings, too. Plateaus that seemed like overthinking, or creative blocks, or stagnation. I felt one rise when I imagined what it would take to help 1,000 entrepreneurs scale to 8 figures and give away $1 million each to their favorite cause. That's a billion dollars of impact. A vision I can't unsee. And the moment I touched it, all my old doubts flooded back.

*Why me? Why now? What if I'm asking for too much?*

But that's the nature of growth. Each new level reveals beliefs that no longer serve us. They come up because they're ready to be replaced. And they remind me why I continue on this journey.

Because I am called. And so are you.

You're not just building a business. You're answering something deeper. You're responding to a knowing that lives inside you; a truth that refuses to be ignored.

That's what this book is about. Not just scaling to 8 figures or building a large business, but becoming someone who can manage it all with integrity and ease. Someone who doesn't lose themselves along the way. Someone who leads with wholeness.

The spiral won't always be smooth, but it will always move you forward. It will shape your leadership. It will sharpen your discernment. It will expose the constraints that are no longer yours to carry.

You'll face hard decisions. You'll want to give up. You'll doubt yourself. But if you stay, if you reflect, rewire, and let go, you will rise. And when you do, you won't rise alone. You'll bring others with you.

That's what happened to me.

The process of becoming my future self, the woman I envisioned, created a new elegance that anchored me in wholeness. I didn't expect that would be the gift of building an 8-figure business. But it was.

And this is where the spiral hands you off to structure. Because while the inner world shapes who you become, the outer world still needs a framework.

Let's talk about the stages of your business, and the systems that help you retain what you've earned.

# CHAPTER 2

# THE FIRE YOURSELF FRAMEWORK™
# THE FOUR STAGES OF EVERY BUSINESS

The numbers don't lie: 96% of businesses never hit $1 million in revenue, and 50% fail within the first five years.

The odds aren't just stacked, they're sobering. Most founders never reach scale, let alone exit successfully. Not because they lack drive or their idea isn't good, but because they never learn how to grow and scale their business without burning out in the process.

After Katelyn's accident in 2012, I believed I had to choose between caring for her and keeping my business dream alive. At that time, my thinking was flawed: If I chose my daughter, my business would fail. I convinced myself it was an either-or scenario, the kind of black-and-white thinking born from trauma. So I chose. Of course, I chose her.

But in making the decision to stay home, and intentionally stay away from the office, I saw something I hadn't allowed myself to see before. My team stepped up. They took initiative and made decisions without me. They handled clients, calls, and issues I once managed myself. Because I stayed true to my core value of family, the result was that a year and a half later, my business had doubled.

At that moment, I didn't see that outcome coming. I truly believed my business would fail because I was choosing to be a mom over being a CEO. But as Katelyn (and my parents) made a full recovery and grew into the bright, beautiful young woman she is today, I began to see that life, and business, could still move forward.

The time away from the office and giving my team the chance to shine, then seeing the actual numbers doubling our revenue, that was the moment everything changed. I was the problem.

And that marked the ending of how I had always operated. I wish it would have changed overnight, like I could snap my fingers and presto, the lesson would be integrated. But that wasn't to be my path, or spiral.

During this season, I brought on two exceptional team members who made a huge difference. I was no longer the only financial advisor bringing in new clients and generating revenue. But once Katelyn was fully recovered, I slipped back into old habits. Even with proof of my team's ability, I kept trying to control everything.

And, yes, on paper, everything looked like a win. But inside, I was still exhausted. The speed that once felt electric now felt suffocating. I had created the systems, but I didn't create the space for me to breathe, explore, and lead. I was still doing and holding too much. I was still wired to Hustle.

Finally, the lesson hit home: the business was evolving, but I hadn't changed. I upgraded the strategies but not myself; I had stalled in the spiral. And no matter how sexy the numbers looked, the way I was leading wasn't sustainable.

Most entrepreneurs miss this key moment. They track revenue. They track team size. They build better systems. But they neglect upgrading the identity that should lead it all. When your internal world can't handle what your external world is creating, everything starts to wobble. You stall. You second-guess. You start controlling more. You self-sabotage.

That's why I created the Fire Yourself Framework™ — the foundation of this book. It's the step-by-step process to scale to 8 figures, simplify growth, and evolve into the version of yourself you've always envisioned. No matter the industry, product, or service, the pattern is universal. Every successful entrepreneur progresses through four external stages that are structural, observable, and measurable.

Hustle.
Surrender.
Harmony.
Legacy.

These are operational thresholds, each with its own revenue range, team structure, and strategic requirements. But they're also deeply tied to the evolution of the entrepreneur at the core.

The Entrepreneurial Spiral™ illustrates your internal ascent. These four stages serve as mirrors and tools for measuring your business growth. Understanding the difference, and combining both, is how you create something sustainable, scalable, and truly aligned.

Let's start at the beginning: Hustle.

## Hustle

**Revenue:** Up to $1 million or until you Surrender. **Team:** You, you and a few assistants, and/or independent contractors. **Structure:**

Scrappy, chaotic energy. It's messy, and that's ok as it can take you to your first million.

Hustle is where the dream gets built with whatever tools you have. It's all-in energy. Long nights, lots of coffee, and, sometimes, unpaid invoices. You're selling, delivering, learning, experimenting, and solving problems on the fly. You're doing it yourself, or with a tiny team, because there's no other choice.

Most entrepreneurs at this stage earn less than a million in annual revenue, with a small team. There are no real systems in place. You are the system.

When I started my business, I stayed in this stage longer than I should have.

I said yes to every opportunity. I booked thirty appointments each week. I skipped lunch, responded to emails at midnight, and was still cleaning out the office fridge. I gave every ounce of energy to building something that could support me should the worst outcome of a tense marriage transpire, and I didn't pause long enough to ask if it was sustainable.

That's the nature of Hustle. It's not meant to be balanced; it's meant to ignite the engine.

Hustle isn't bad. It's powerful. It's the fire that gets you off the ground. It's how you build momentum when all you have is belief and grit. But it has a limited shelf life. It's not meant to last forever. And the longer you stay here, the more your business depends on your effort to survive.

Hustle provided me traction. But it also turned into a trap.

That's the risk at this stage. Hustle works, until it doesn't. It creates momentum, but it's not sustainable. You are the engine of the business, and when you stop, everything stops with you.

Most entrepreneurs in Hustle face an invisible glass ceiling they can't name: the idea that working harder is the only way to succeed. They believe that if they slow down, everything will fall apart.

And yet, Hustle is the foundation. It's where you find your voice, build resilience, and you stretch your capacity to serve. It's a powerful stage, but only when you see it as a phase, not an identity or a badge of honor.

The goal of Hustle is not to escape it quickly. The goal is to learn what you need to understand without lingering longer than necessary.

Because when you're ready to grow, the next stage will require something completely different.

## Surrender

**Revenue:** $1–$3M. **Team:** 4–10+ people. **Structure:** Systems and other leaders emerging, but still founder-dependent.

Surrender begins when you hit your limit. You've built something real. Revenue is increasing, usually somewhere in the $1 million to $3 million mark. Clients and sales are coming in steadily. The work is good. But you've reached the point where you can't handle it on your own.

This is where many entrepreneurs begin to feel like they're failing, not because they're losing business, but because they can't handle everything anymore. It feels like burnout, but it's really a bandwidth crisis. The business has surpassed your personal energy.

Surrender is the stage where you learn to lead. Not by doing more, but by letting go. By developing the team and systems to handle what you no longer can or should not carry.

This is where you start making decisions based on vision instead of reaction. Where you stop solving every problem yourself, start developing other leaders, and create a structure that operates without you in the room.

But Surrender isn't easy. It requires trust, first in others, but more importantly, in yourself. It asks you to loosen your grip on control, to unhook your worth from being the hero, and to step back so the business can breathe.

When I first moved into this stage, I still had one foot in Hustle. I would delegate tasks but then micromanage to ensure they got done my way. I hired people but didn't empower them. I wanted help but didn't know how to accept it without feeling like I was slacking.

This stage is about identity as much as it is about operations. You stop being the doer and start becoming the leader. And once you make that shift, everything changes.

You reclaim your time. You clarify your role. And for the first time, you create space.

That's what unlocks the door to the third stage: Harmony.

## Harmony

**Revenue:** $3M–$5M+. **Team:** 10–15+ people. **Structure:** Systems optimized, team empowered, founder in visionary role.

Harmony is the phase when the business begins to feel spacious, the "Pinch Me!" stage in business. You've built the systems. You've empowered the team. And now, the business can operate without your constant involvement.

Most Harmony-stage businesses generate $3 to $5 million or more in revenue, and have an executive team in place. There's operational maturity here. Weekly meetings. Dashboards and Key Performance Indicators (KPIs). Strategic plans.

This is where alignment begins to feel more embodied. You set boundaries around your time. You trust your leadership. You make decisions with purpose instead of urgency.

The energy of this stage is not passive, it's powerful. It's where you do less, but lead more. Where clarity is your currency and your business begins to compound because it's finally structured to scale.

But Harmony can come with its own plateau. When things feel good, it's tempting to believe that you've gone as far as you can.

This is the season to ask the bigger questions about what comes next, not just for the business, but for your Legacy and how you might influence and impact this world. Because the final stage isn't about having more. It's about finding meaning.

## Legacy

**Revenue:** $5M–$10M+ and more. **Team:** 15-20+ team members and/or distributed leadership across multiple departments. **Structure:** The company runs without your day-to-day involvement. Wealth multiplies through people, Intellectual Property (IP), and platform.

Legacy is the rarest stage. It's where impact extends beyond your direct involvement. It's where your business becomes a platform for others to succeed, not just a vessel for your own success.

Most Legacy businesses are at or approaching the $10 million mark and beyond. But this isn't about just revenue or enterprise value. It's about the underlying structure. You're no longer the face of every offer, nor are you central to the day-to-day.

This stage is about designing yourself out of the center, not because you're stepping back, but because you've built something that can stand without you. It's about creating wealth that flows through you, not just to you. About elevating others, funding causes, and multiplying your reach without increasing your hours.

But Legacy doesn't happen by accident. It requires vision, people, structure, and a level of trust that only comes from doing the work in the first three stages. You don't reach Legacy by sprinting. You get there by surrendering, integrating, and choosing alignment over ego.

This is where the spiral and the structure intersect. Where inner coherence meets outer impact. Where you stop building just for success, and start building for significance.

Because Legacy isn't something you leave behind. It's something you get to live.

## The Sweet Life

Most entrepreneurs never reach Legacy, not because they lacked the dream, but because they burned out before getting a chance to live it. I almost did, too.

Back in 2014, everything on the outside said I'd made it. We had doubled our revenue. I'd built the machine, but I was still the engine. I hadn't yet learned to trust my team, to let go of control, or to allow the business to breathe without me holding it up.

That moment nearly broke me, but it also showed me something I wouldn't forget:

*Growth wasn't about pushing harder. It was about learning to lead differently.*

Each stage—Hustle, Surrender, Harmony, Legacy—demanded something new from me. And I didn't always know how to give it. I fought Surrender. I resisted Harmony. I kept one foot in Hustle because it felt safer to run on adrenaline than to face what was underneath. But every time I hit the edge of my capacity, the spiral appeared. The patterns reemerged. And I had a choice: repeat what I'd done before or rise into something new.

The first time I realized I couldn't keep going the way I was came shortly after Katelyn's accident. It didn't hit me in a moment of crisis or panic, but felt more like a soft, gentle, persistent knowing tugging at my heart. And one day, I was just... done. I'd hit my wall. And in that stillness, I heard the question I'd been avoiding: *What are you building, and at what cost?*

That question changed everything because I didn't want a business that operated on exhaustion. I wanted one that reflected who I was becoming: strong, clear, deeply resourced, and free.

This is what most entrepreneurs overlook. They focus so much on growing the business that they forget to develop the version of themselves who can truly lead it. When your internal world can't hold what your external world is creating, the structure will eventually break, as I have experienced.

This is why understanding these four stages is important. Not because they're trendy or conceptual, but because they serve as the real roadmap to sustainable growth. I've experienced it firsthand and advised it to many of my private entrepreneurial clients and, now, you.

They are the structural milestones that tell you where you are and what's required next. And when you connect them with the internal growth of the spiral, you don't just expand your business, you become the kind of leader who can manage it, scale it, and keep it going.

You don't need to race through these stages. You don't need to show strength or pretend clarity. Just keep moving forward; the spiral will meet you where you are.

When you rise with internal intention, team support, and alignment of your integrity, you don't just build a business. You create a Legacy that reflects who you are and everything you've grown through to get here.

Let's go.

# PART ONE: HUSTLE

## The Hustle Process

# CHAPTER 3

## WIRED WEIRD

It started early for me. My brother Rick and I used to wait for the perfect moment in the Seattle summer when the suburban sun finally showed up, and new neighborhoods under construction buzzed with workers. We'd set up our Country Time Lemonade stands right at the edge of the development zone and charge 50 cents a cup. We knew exactly when to be there. In pigtails and jelly shoes, I came to understand our market.

And that wasn't the only hustle. My father was a pilot, which meant we often flew standby with long layovers, and, yes, I knew every city airport code by heart. At MSP, while our parents waited at the gate, Rick and I would dash out to the parking garage to round up every stray luggage cart we could find, returning them for pocket change. We mowed lawns. We babysat. We did whatever it took to make money, not because we had to, but because it lit us up. This was fun for us. That surge of energy from solving a problem and making a buck was electric. It was in my blood.

My mom would drive us to Southcenter Mall after a long week and let us roam. Acid-washed jeans, banana clips, and the scent of Cinnabon in the air were the vibe but Wet Seal was the only place to be. I'd spend my hard-earned quarters on something small and sparkly, because I earned it. With NKOTB blasting in my Walkman, I felt like a boss and the coolest kid ever!

Entrepreneurship isn't something I learned, it's something I am. But not everyone in my family has that wiring. One of my brothers is a musician, and while his path is beautiful in its own right, that entrepreneurial engine didn't hum for him the same way it did for Rick and me. That's the thing about entrepreneurship: the path chooses us. We see the world through a different lens.

Entrepreneurs are simply wired differently. *We just are*. We see possibilities where others see chaos. Someone else might glance at a messy client intake form and feel overwhelmed by the half-filled answers, vague goals, and lack of clarity. But you instinctively know: *this person just needs a process. A path. A plan*. You already see the solution, the outcome, the transformation, even before it's fully articulated. That's how we're wired.

Some entrepreneurs are born in childhood, like me, while others rise from rock-bottom moments that leave them broke and broken. Some experience that lightning bolt of "Eureka!", the spark of a new idea that catches fire or the feeling of being pulled by a higher power. Many are shaped by all of it; a mix of survival, inspiration, and moments that build slowly over time into something undeniable. The source of entrepreneurship is as vast and complex as life itself. But the truth is this: you are wired to see potential, to create, and to build. That instinct is natural.

For me, being an entrepreneur and a founder feels both like a deep responsibility and a connection to something greater than myself. I've heard my private entrepreneurial clients and friends describe it as a call to something higher, a pull that's hard to explain, and a drive that is nothing short of supernatural.

Pretty cool, if you ask me.

But that is also *your* wiring. It's what fuels that first big push; the all-in energy that says, *What if... ? Let's do it!* and *Jump!* all in the same breath. Or, what I call, Hustle.

Hustle is the birthplace of your business. It's filled with passion, grit, and courage. But staying here too long can lead to burnout, control issues, and lots of money guilt. Hustle gets you started, but it cannot and will not carry you all the way to where you want to go: Freedom. Hustle is a stage of intensity that includes long nights with mindless midnight snacks, DIY sprints with Pomodoro Timers, audiobooks or podcasts on self-development playing in the background as you bathe, cook, and "take a break." But most of all, Hustle is about proving yourself.

This is the spark. That small, tiny fire that gets you started, and requires constant oxygen and fuel to keep burning. Hustle is part of your magic. It's what built your business, helped you launch, and brought in your first wave of success.

You love it. You crave it. It's your superpower and your young baby all wrapped into one beautiful business.

But when Hustle turns into your home instead of your launchpad, it begins to cost you.

# CHAPTER 4

# THE HUSTLE MINDSET

In late 2000, I found my wedding guest list. That database was four years old and the foundation for my new business. No fancy software, just a dial-up modem, a kitchen table, and a drive that was unstoppable. I sat at that table and typed every single pitch letter in WordPerfect. I told them I was starting my own financial advising firm and asked them to meet with me or send someone my way. That's how it all started.

I had been told by my former broker-dealer that if I kept my head down, worked hard, and waited for another advisor to leave, I could become an advisor in about 10 years. Honestly, I was frustrated. I was 23 years old, I had little experience, a solid reputation, and most importantly, I wanted to be a financial advisor rather than support one.

So, I did exactly that. I left my 9-5 job to start my own business so that I could work 24/7. Welcome to Hustle, folks.

I needed, and desperately wanted, to make my own money. I believed that if I could just build something successful, if I could become financially independent, then maybe I'd feel better. Maybe I'd feel free. Maybe I'd feel good enough.

But the deeper truth was harder to say out loud. I didn't feel accepted. I didn't feel worthy. I didn't feel important or valued. I didn't feel good enough. I didn't feel like my husband wanted me. I felt invisible in my own life.

And, of course, underneath all of that, I felt like shit.

So, I threw my hands up to the sky and said, *Forget all of you. I'm going to frickin' figure this out.* The "this" being financial freedom. Because in my place of pain, my place of loneliness, that was the only freedom I thought could give me peace.

That moment wasn't about ambition; it was about survival. I needed something to hold onto, something that would love me back or, at the very least, give me a sense of control and validation. So, I turned to the one thing I knew would respond to my effort. *My business.*

I poured everything I had into building it. I invested my time, energy, and identity. The Hustle became my lifeline. It gave me a reason to get out of bed. It gave me a place to channel all my pain. And as it turns out, I loved the work. I loved helping people. It gave me a sense of purpose, a reason to keep moving forward. But more than anything, it made me feel important.

And it gave me something else: a welcomed distraction from the parts of my personal life I wasn't ready to face.

Because the frustration and unspoken pain I experienced in my young adulthood had planted something in me; a deep-rooted belief that I wasn't enough. That mindset shaped how I worked, how I led, and how I chased achievement. For the next twelve years, I let it drive me.

## Hustle. And when it's really bad.

"Hell no!" he said with exasperation after I asked him if he flew his team around on his newly acquired private jet.

We were sitting at a long table in Salt Lake City, surrounded by top advisors and founders, and I had just met Jamie. We connected immediately. Both of us knew what it meant to grow fast, to go all in, and to carry the weight of a business on your back. He was brilliant and a natural entrepreneur. If I had lemonstands, Jamie was hustling bikes when he was eight years old. So when he told me he'd bought the jet, I asked the natural follow-up.

"Do you fly your team around with it?"

That's when he told me that no one, not even his staff or top leadership, even knew he had it. It was in the vault.

I blinked. "Wait. Why—do you feel guilty?"

He paused. He hadn't really thought about it, but the truth began to surface. It didn't feel safe to share; he didn't want to risk judgment from those closest to him, so he kept it to himself. This incredible, beautiful reward, and he tucked it away as if it was something to be ashamed of.

I already knew this in my bones: you can work your ass off, build something incredible, and still feel like you have to hide the win.

I recognized it in him because I had experienced it.

This is toxic Hustle. And it's not a place I want you to call home.

At my peak, I handled over thirty client appointments a week, hosted marketing seminars, managed everything myself, returned emails during dinner, and finalized paperwork I could have delegated. I was the bottleneck, the engine, the fixer, the closer. I wore it like a badge of honor because the busier I was, the more important I felt. But the truth was I was running away from my marriage, my emotions, and my own sense of inadequacy.

Mine looked like more grind, more grit, and then giving myself a reward through retail therapy that I hid from my husband. It was a release for all the time, energy, and focus I put into my business. If I knew I'd be paid a big commission on the 15th, by the night of the 14th, I had already filled my cart with luxury designer clothes, purses, and shoes. Jamie bought a jet and wouldn't tell a soul. I bought Louboutins and called it self-care.

But Claire wanted something different.

Her toxic Hustle seemed like overexposure rather than overspending. She was smart, electric, and completely tapped out. As a single mother raising five kids, she traveled nonstop during the weeks she didn't have them, conference after conference, mastermind after mastermind, always chasing the next hit of connection, momentum, and validation. She wasn't focusing on sustainability. She was exhausting herself and burning out every new hire she brought on board. Claire has many things, but patience or focus were not among them. She once told me, half-laughing, that she woke up in a hotel room with a man wearing a court-ordered ankle monitor, and a week later, she had an STD. It sounded like a punchline. But beneath that, I sensed her pain because it was strikingly familiar to what I had gone through. She was distracting herself from her reality by outworking her loneliness.

Toxic Hustle is what happens when that incredible drive you have, the one that helps you build, expand, and see beyond the ordinary, gets hijacked. When your vision and execution start diverting energy toward mere survival instead of strategic growth.

All of us, Jamie, Claire, and I, wore different versions of the same mask: Prove. Perform. Reward. Hide. Repeat. The inverse of the Entrepreneurial Spiral™.

I've seen clients dig financial graves trying to offset their burnout. They buy stretch houses that turn into stress houses. They justify the upgraded car as a deduction. Not because they're being irresponsible, but because they're burned out and trying to feel better. Overspending becomes the reward for going fast. They make decisions without processing and spend without being present as they sign on the line or hit the "Purchase" button. They don't feel it. They just *do* it. And that's the difference. It's not that any of this is right or wrong. *It's the absence of awareness that makes it toxic.*

Toxic Hustle performs beautifully, but it will never give you the rare air you seek.

There's another way, though. That's where we're headed next.

## Hustle. And why it's not bad.

Let's be clear—Hustle ain't bad.

It's how I got started. That season at the kitchen table, writing letters to our wedding guest list and asking people to meet with me, that was Hustle. Saying yes to a client before I had a system in place, that was Hustle. Building something from scratch with no roadmap, just drive, that was pure Hustle.

And I wouldn't change it.

Hustle is where big things start. It's the garage startup. The early mornings. The late nights. The steep learning curve. The full-hearted belief that what you're building matters. That momentum builds something real.

And it works. Especially in the beginning. You can go fast when it's just you.

Most entrepreneurs stay in Hustle too long. Not because they want to, but because they can't see another way.

There's a kind of Hustle that stems from your values and integrity. And there's a kind that feeds on pressure, fear, and old habits.

On the surface, they look the same. But one expands you. The other will absolutely empty you.

When Hustle is rooted in your values, it builds something that lasts. It aligns your effort with your vision. It energizes you. It brings momentum that feels sustainable. Hustle will get you here, but aligning with your values is what carries you forward.

So, let's go back to when you first started your business.

# CHAPTER 5

# HUSTLE TOOLS

## Remembering the Magic

Where were you when you first had the idea for your business? Do you remember the moment you thought, "I can solve this," or "This idea could change everything?"

Mine happened when I was working at the bank and was a whopping 22 years old. The standard way of treating customers was transactional at best and indifferent at worst; a polite but distant, "You can call us, we're here," without ever going beyond that. It was an attitude and a way of doing business that would never allow employees to see that each customer was a person with a life full of meaning, dreams, and goals.

I hated it.

I wanted to help these people and build lasting relationships with them, aka clients for life. And I knew I could help them pursue financial independence. I knew I could be that activator, that guide, that helper. I didn't care if it was getting out of debt, helping them max out a college fund for their newborn child, or talking them through investment strategies. I wanted to partner with them. I wanted to collaborate with them on some of the most important decisions they needed to make in their lives: what to do with their money.

What was that for you? Was it a flash of possibility? The client you couldn't stop thinking about? The pull in your gut to build something better? What was the moment a door opened in your mind and you walked through it? Because every superhero has an origin story.

And that start was never just a strategy; it was a vision of something different and better. And even now, years later, that original vision will most likely still be calling to you. Sure, it's shifted, and the colors might be brighter, but it remains. So, let's bring it out to the person you are today.

Imagine I give you a magic wand, or whatever you need to feel limitless, and tap into your most precious resource: your imagination. This is the time I am asking you to expand your mind into thinking something you are not currently living. It can be uncomfortable. So, it doesn't matter if you use a magic wand, a four-leaf clover, or a genie in a bottle, just erase the limits of your current situation.

If you could wave a magic wand over your business and life, what would change instantly?


Where are you spending your time?

What are you no longer tolerating?

What does success feel like in your body?

This isn't fantasy. It's attunement to what you truly desire: When you can name what you really want, stop chasing what you never needed, and find the sweet spot of *enough*.

For me, enough means being present with my family while growing a business that empowers entrepreneurs who are here to scale with purpose and make a positive impact on our world. It looks like unplugged days, traveling the world, and a company that thrives without my constant oversight. It feels and looks like an overflow; it feels like freedom.

Back when I was "Hustling", this vision of my life was unimaginable. It was somewhere... out there. I only reached this point because I cast a vision for what I truly desired. Funny, considering how impossible it felt then. The vision didn't materialize the next day, even though that would have been wonderful. Over time, the future I'd pictured came into focus once my values supported it.

*Your vision defines what you're building. Your values define how you build it.*

Without that connection to the most vital parts of your being, toxic Hustle takes over. You begin grinding out of fear instead of leading with clarity. You confuse movement for progress. And over time, the business you built starts controlling you.

Values are the antidote.

They're not fluff or just another exercise in a book. They're your anchors. When you understand them, use them, and act from them, everything, and I mean everything, works in your life. Your boundaries, your calendar, your energy, your team. You lead differently. You love differently. And you live a life that's meaningful to you.

So, before you build what's next, let's name what matters most.

## Personal Core Values

We're starting with *your* personal values.

If your Hustle feels off and leaves you wondering, "Is this all there is?" This is where you find out why. If it's flowing, this is how you make it sustainable.

Core values are the unchanging beliefs that guide how you live, lead, and ultimately, build your business. They might look good on a post-it, wallpaper, or website that you never look at, but when used effectively, they become the lifeblood of your world.

Because here's the uncomfortable truth no one admits at the networking mixer: Operating from personal values is both a lagging *and* leading indicator of entrepreneurial growth.

This isn't just mindset work; it's metrics for your business.

Here's how working hard might come from positive core values like the following:

- **Excellence:** I strive for excellence in everything I do, maintaining high standards.
- **Responsibility:** I take ownership for the outcomes and the people who depend on me.

- **Achievement**: I value growth, success, and making a meaningful impact.
- **Service**: I want to help others, so I keep showing up.

In contrast, when Hustle comes from a toxic place, it can also serve as a copying mechanism. This shows up as:

- **Need for control**: If I stop, everything might fall apart.
- **Need for significance**: If I perform, I'll finally be enough.
- **Scarcity mindset**: If I don't push now, the opportunity might disappear.
- **Need for validation**: Where love is earned through achievement.

They both influence our behaviors, but core values energize you and foster sustainable success. When fear, scarcity, or old mental mindsets dominate, toxic Hustle will drain you and keep you stuck in a cycle of burnout, forcing you to repeatedly prove you're enough.

## Discover Your Personal Core Values

**Instructions:**

**Step 1:** Read through the list of core values below.

**Step 2:** Circle or highlight any values that truly resonate with you, values that feel authentic to who you are, and not who you think you *should* be. Pick as many as you want.

| | | | | |
|---|---|---|---|---|
| Accountability | Achievement | Adventure | Authenticity | Balance |
| Beauty | Belonging | Challenge | Collaboration | Commitment |
| Community | Compassion | Connection | Contribution | Courage |
| Creativity | Curiosity | Determination | Devotion | Discipline |

| | | | | |
|---|---|---|---|---|
| Diversity | Empathy | Encouragement | Equality | Excellence |
| Faith | Family | Flexibility | Forgiveness | Freedom |
| Fun | Generosity | Grace | Gratitude | Growth |
| Harmony | Honesty | Honor | Hope | Humor |
| Impact | Independence | Innovation | Integrity | Intimacy |
| Joy | Justice | Kindness | Leadership | Learning |
| Legacy | Listening | Love | Loyalty | Mastery |
| Mindfulness | Openness | Optimism | Order | Passion |
| Patience | Peace | Perseverance | Play | Presence |
| Prosperity | Purpose | Reflection | Respect | Responsibility |
| Security | Self-Expression | Service | Simplicity | Spirituality |
| Spontaneity | Stability | Stewardship | Strength | Success |
| Support | Surrender | Sustainability | Teamwork | Time |
| Tradition | Transformation | Trust | Truth | Vision |
| Vitality | Vulnerability | Wealth | Wisdom | Wonder |

**Step 3:** Next, narrow down your core values circled to your Top 5.

To do this, picture yourself at an amazing party. The energy is electric. The food is top-notch. And you look incredible! The room is packed with everyone who matters: your clients, your team, your friends, your family. All of them.

Suddenly, you hear the clink of silverware against a champagne glass. You turn and see your ride-or-die, your favorite person, standing with a glass raised, calling for the room's attention. They're about to give a toast. And, plot twist, it's for you. This is completely unexpected, but the words are coming straight from their heart. As they speak, they name five qualities that define you. Five things they admire most. Five values you consistently embody. These are the values you're known for. The ones that make people trust you, follow you, love you. What are they? Those are your five.

1. _____
2. _____
3. _____
4. _____
5. _____

**Step 4:** From your five core values, write down one to three examples of how you've embodied them in the past 90 days. These don't need to be loud or public-facing. But they do need to be real. Maybe it was how you spoke to yourself during a tough week. Maybe it was the way you handled a difficult conversation with grace. Maybe it was letting go of a team member in a way that honored your standards and their dignity. Big or small, these moments count.

_____
_____
_____
_____
_____
_____
_____

**Step 5:** Reflect: If you're struggling to find examples, pause here. What's missing: courage or clarity? Or are the values you wrote down still tied to who you think you should be? Are you living in alignment with these values right now? Is each one based on love or fear? Is this who you truly are, or who you've been conditioned to become?

_____

_____

_____

_____

_____

_____

_____

_____

_____

_____

_____

_____

# CHAPTER 6

# THE HUSTLE AUDIT™

## Your Business Vitals

Marcus came to me completely burned out.

His goal was to make $10 million in revenue and he was fully capable of hitting that mark, but his business was running him. He was smart, and an exceptional physical therapist, but no matter how much he earned, it never quite felt like enough. Where does all the money go?

We mapped out his week. Every therapy session, every call and email, every task he still touched, even those he supposedly delegated. The late-night follow-ups. The "tiny" client favors. The meetings he didn't need to attend, but couldn't seem to skip.

And there it was: the story of his beliefs about control, worth, time, money, his staff, and how success is supposed to feel.

Your schedule never lies.

Marcus hired a team and generated consistent revenue. But he white knuckled his calendar and therefore, his business. He was still doing *everything* and made himself the irreplaceable bottleneck.

This is what Hustle does when left unchecked: it weaves itself into your systems, your schedule, your identity. It proudly wears a thousand different masks—commitment, responsibility, high standards—and convinces you that this is what it means to lead, and be successful.

But if you're doing everything, you're not leading. You're surviving.

The Hustle Audit™ isn't busywork. It's a mirror.

It reveals the truth about where your energy is going, and whether it aligns with your values and the business you're trying to build.

## Tool: The Hustle Audit™

### Step 1: Inventory Your Hustle

Using the worksheet provided, start by writing down all the activities that fill your day, every day, for 10 days, including the weekend. Enter all your activities and roles as the leader of your business, including tasks like emails, research, social media, and client meetings, as well as personal responsibilities such as taking the kids to sports practice, grocery shopping, and date night. Essentially, everything you do in both your business and personal life.

Be honest. Be thorough. Don't overlook the "small stuff" because *those* are often the biggest energy leaks. This is a reflection, not a judgment. Just observe what you're thinking as you keep track everything!

# INVENTORY YOUR HUSTLE

| Time (Start\End/Total) | Role/Task/Activity | Frequency Daily (d), Weekly (W), Monthly (M) | Energy Level (♥,✅,✕) | Notes/Reflections |
|---|---|---|---|---|
| 5:00-5:30am | | | | |
| 5:30-6:00am | | | | |
| 6:00-6:30am | | | | |
| 6:30-7:00am | | | | |
| 7:00-7:30am | | | | |
| 7:30-8:00am | | | | |
| 8:00-8:30am | | | | |
| 8:30-9:00am | | | | |
| 9:00-9:30am | | | | |
| 9:30-10:00am | | | | |
| 10:00-10:30am | | | | |
| 10:30-11:00am | | | | |
| 11:00-11:30am | | | | |
| 11:30-12:00pm | | | | |
| 12:00-12:30pm | | | | |
| 12:30-1:00pm | | | | |
| 1:00-1:30pm | | | | |
| 1:30-2:00pm | | | | |
| 2:00-2:30pm | | | | |
| 2:30-3:00pm | | | | |
| 3:00-3:30pm | | | | |
| 3:30-4:00pm | | | | |
| 4:00-4:30pm | | | | |
| 4:30-5:00pm | | | | |
| 5:00-5:30pm | | | | |
| 5:30-6:00pm | | | | |
| 6:00-6:30pm | | | | |
| 6:30-7:00pm | | | | |
| 7:00-7:30pm | | | | |
| 7:30-8:00pm | | | | |
| 8:00-8:30pm | | | | |
| 8:30-9:00pm | | | | |
| 9:00-9:30pm | | | | |
| 9:30-10:00pm | | | | |
| 10:00-10:30pm | | | | |
| 10:30-11:00pm | | | | |

To use a digital version of the hustle inventory please visit my book resource page at www.thejuliacarlson.com/books or scan QR code here.

## Step 2: Your Superpower Zone

Look at your list. Really look at it.

These are the tasks, activities, habits, responsibilities, and mental loads you carry in your business and life. Some are big, some feel small. But every single one takes energy. That's what we're tracking next.

In the energy level column of your audit, begin labeling how each task actually makes you feel with the following:

*LOVE*: It gives you life. You'd do it all day. It's energizing, expansive, and magnetic.

*LIKE*: You're good at it. You don't mind it. It's fine, but it's not your zone of genius.

*DISLIKE*: It drains you. It depletes you. You dread it, avoid it, or collapse after doing it. My friend calls these "Energy Vampires."

If you're not sure, zoom out. Ask yourself: over the past week or month, does this energize me or empty me? That is the question you need to ask yourself every day.

And if the answer still isn't clear, consult your Future Self.

## Step 3: Your Future Self Knows

Imagine it's 12 months from now. You've scaled. You've stepped into leadership. You've designed a business that no longer requires your fingerprints on every file.

Now ask:

Where are you spending your time?

What have you let go of?

What roles no longer belong to you?

What's been delegated, automated, or eliminated?

Let this version of you, the one who's no longer in survival mode, show you the truth. Because if your time doesn't match the business you say you're building, it's time to realign.

## Step 4: Hustle Insights

Now look at the patterns.

- Are you clinging to tasks that could be delegated?
- Are you still the default decision-maker in every situation?
- Is your energy focused on the highest, best use of your gifts, or is it going to whatever's loudest?
- And most importantly, do you believe your presence is the only thing keeping this business alive?

This is where most entrepreneurs struggle. Not because they don't know how to grow, but because they've built a business that relies too heavily on them.

I know this because I did it. Katelyn's life-threatening car accident woke me up to what mattered. It showed me what I'd built, a business that could run without me, if only I would let it. Every email, every decision, every dollar... I was at the center of it all.

And part of me liked it that way.

Because when you're always needed, you feel important. You feel irreplaceable. But being irreplaceable is a cage. That moment forced me to ask: why had I built something that would fall apart without me?

Which brings us to this next part.

**You Are the Bottleneck. But You Don't Have to Stay There.**

Not every Hustle is toxic.

You can be in a high-growth season and still stay aligned. You can love working hard and still operate from your vision.

But the moment Hustle becomes your identity... the moment everything rests on you... the moment you start confusing exhaustion with excellence.

That's when you know you're the bottleneck.

Here are some warning signs:

- You approve every piece of content, invoice, or idea.
- Your team can't make a decision without running it past you.
- You're still on every group text, call, or client issue.
- You dread stepping away because things unravel in your absence.
- You're trapped in reactivity: too busy to delegate, too tired to scale.

It's not always fear or trauma. Sometimes, it's just habit.

But this is your invitation to pause and observe it. See how much you are doing and why you might be so exhausted. Because once you recognize it, you can let it go.

The Hustle Audit™ isn't about doing less just for the sake of it. It's about focusing on what matters most, with clarity, purpose, and power.

## Seasons Planning - Find Your Focus Every 90 Days

During one season of my business, I gave up all my profit for 90 days. Every last dollar was reinvested into new technology, team hires, and infrastructure. Not because I had to, but because I knew what I wanted to create. I saw the future, and I was willing to trade short-term gain for long-term momentum. That decision shaped everything.

Looking back, that wasn't sacrifice; it was focus. It was how I started growing my business in 90-day seasons of focus.

Most entrepreneurs don't stall because they're not trying hard enough. They stall because they're juggling too many things at once. The Hustle Audit™ likely revealed this—how many roles you still carry, how much noise you manage, and how little space is left for your true genius. That's where the next shift begins: with seasons.

Just like nature, business can move in seasons, and each one calls for a different kind of focus. You get to choose what matters most in each season, but the real discipline is saying no to what doesn't fit right now.

To this day, I still run my business in 90-day seasons, and it's the format that I've used for the past decade. When I was in Hustle, each quarter had just one priority, because that's all I could handle, even if I was hiring independent contractors to support me.

Now that I am living the dream in both Harmony and Legacy, we have 3-5 priorities per 90-day season because my executive team is an all-star crew that can handle more than when I was going solo in the Hustle. And if you're in Hustle, focusing on one priority per 90-day season is the secret sauce to making progress. Will it be hard to say no to every shiny object that comes your way? Yup, it will be, and I remember that constant whisper of anxiety in my mind saying, *"I'm missing out. I'm behind."*

But, I had made the decision to cut off everything that didn't support that one goal, that singular focus. It was painful not to invest in everything I wanted at that very moment, but I knew that the gains were on the other side of focus. So, everything else was postponed, I gained serious ground, and suddenly I was no longer interested in doing it all. I was interested in doing the right things, in the right order, with the right energy behind them.

If you've been sprinting without direction, or grinding without clarity, it's time to bring order to your effort and focus everything on the one thing that will make the biggest impact. That starts now.

Use your Hustle Audit to answer these questions:

1.  What are you still doing that someone else could handle with the proper guidance?

2.  What drains you but keeps showing up on your calendar?

3.  What are you holding onto out of fear rather than fact?

Then make your first moves. Just three small shifts. Think of them like compound interest; unremarkable at first, but powerful over time. Choose one thing to delegate, one thing to automate, and one thing to eliminate as you focus on one big priority over the next 90 days.

At different stages, the size of your moves will evolve. Early on, one strategic decision—a single product or service you phase out, a new piece of technology you integrate, or one task or role you finally hand off—can create real momentum.

As your company grows, your capacity expands. You can make multiple shifts each quarter, focusing on three to five key priorities if you're running a larger organization like mine, or perhaps one meaningful delegation if you're still in an earlier stage. The principle stays the same: steady, intentional action compounds into exponential results.

What is your one focus for the next 90 days?

_____

_____

_____

_____

_____

_____

What will you delegate, automate, or eliminate the next 90 days that supports your focused result?

1. _____

2. _____

3. _____

Because this is how we start leaving the chaos of Hustle and move into the clarity of Surrender, not by doing more, but by doing less, better.

# CHAPTER 7

# HUSTLE MONEY

## Everyday You're Hustlin'

You didn't start a business to go broke. And you definitely didn't start a business to become your own worst boss.

But somewhere along the way, that's what happens. This business isn't just a job. It's your calling. And maybe your most important one, because it fuels everything else. It's the lifeblood that supports your family, your freedom, and the future you're building. You carry the weight of the entire company. You work nonstop, lose sleep, and avoid the numbers, not because there's no money coming in, but because it never feels like enough.

Here's what I've learned: your relationship with money determines how far your business can grow. Before I began working with private entrepreneurial clients through the Fire Yourself Framework™, my clients were the ones who entrusted me with their money as their financial advisor. The ones who experienced the greatest wealth and abundance weren't always the savviest investors, they were the ones with the right mindset. They allowed money to flow, to be shared, to be spent with grounded worthiness. As a financial advisor, I saw it over and over again. The biggest barrier to wealth wasn't strategy or skill. It was a mindset. That truth became the heartbeat of my last book, *Money Loves You*, which I wrote to help people reshape the way they think and feel about money.

The same is true for entrepreneurs, especially founders. Their relationship to money often needs a full-blown reset. I see too many business owners avoiding their finances and not paying themselves a consistent salary. And I get it. Nobody teaches you how to win with money. So, naturally, you avoid it. You weren't taught the rules, you were handed a guilt trip and told to figure it out.

For many, money brings stress. The bills pile up. Arguments at home. There's the pressure to bring in more or the panic of not having enough to make payroll. If money feels heavy, it's because it is. So it makes sense if you've learned to look away. But in business, avoiding it will wreck you. Fast.

Ignoring your numbers doesn't make the fear go away. It feeds it. And as long as you keep feeding the beast, the longer it will live.

This book isn't here to shame you. It's here to help you stare down the fear and build a relationship with money that actually works. One that supports your vision instead of holding it back.

That means we stop glamorizing burnout. We stop wearing scarcity like a badge of honor. No more pride in the struggle. No more quiet suffering. It's time to ditch the money shame because you deserve financial fame and success. And it starts with one thing: paying attention.

Just like your calendar, your numbers never lie. They also tell a story. They reflect what you believe you're worth, and how much you're willing to receive. Yup, this is the point where I say, "Start paying yourself like you mean it."

What comes next is a short money inventory. Nothing fancy. Just a few prompts to honestly assess where you are. These will help you see the patterns you've been living in and how they're holding back your business growth.

Because whether you like it or not, how you relate to money is how you relate to growth.

**On a scale from 1 to 10, how much do you avoid these tasks?**

(1 = I take action right away, 10 = I avoid it completely)

Are you confident in managing your finances, or do you tend to avoid them altogether?

How often do you delay reviewing your numbers or making key financial decisions?

Do you avoid looking at your bank account, bills, or taxes?

Do you manage your finances yourself, or are you ready to delegate this responsibility?

When delegating financial tasks, do you find it easy to trust others, or does letting go feel hard?

Your answers will help you decide if it's time to take more ownership, or finally delegate to the right person or team who can hold this with you.

Because here's the truth most entrepreneurs won't say out loud: We carry silent shame around money. We judge ourselves for not knowing what we were never taught. We feel behind, confused, or like everyone else has it figured out, except us.

If you've been avoiding your finances, feeling confused, or thinking, "I should be better at this by now," you're not alone. Most of us were never taught how to manage money. And that ends here.

Through this book, and through the work we'll do together, whether you choose to DIY it, already work with a financial advisor, or work with me and my team, you'll become financially empowered. You'll move forward with clarity, confidence, and freedom. *Money gets to be safe.* You get to be supported. And this marks the beginning of building wealth that sustains you and the impact you're here to make.

I've seen entrepreneurs with 7-figure businesses still feel stuck when it comes to money. They have the income, but not the ease. And most of the time, it isn't about the numbers, it's about the narrative. Old experiences with money create fear, inadequacy, or that creeping sense of unworthiness. That ends here too.

This is a no-shame zone. No fear. Just truth, clarity, and the tools you need to make the change you've been craving.

You're reading this because you've already built something powerful. You've moved beyond the startup phase. Now, you're ready to scale a sustainable, profitable company. But that next level requires something deeper: clearing out the blocks in your relationship with money so you can actually receive what you've created.

Let's talk about one of those blocks: the myth that you can Hustle your way out of emotional pressure.

Because Hustle isn't just about overworking. It shows up as overspending. It shows up in the impulse to "treat yourself" when the pressure builds, to sign up for the next big thing, to hire the expensive coach, to upgrade the car, the house, or the wardrobe, not from alignment, but from survival. That's not freedom. That's a release valve. And that's the toxic Hustle talking.

It's the same energy that says you can't slow down, that you must grow fast, spend big, stay visible, and prove you're successful at all costs. The same energy that convinces you that if you just keep going, eventually, the stress will subside. But it won't, because it's not about speed, it's about strategy. It's not about how much you make, it's about how you protect what you have and turn your money into wealth.

This is the moment when you choose to live within your means, not as punishment, but as a source of power.

This isn't about tightening your spending so you can't enjoy yourself. It's not about scarcity. It's about alignment. You're allowed to want the beach house and the first-class ticket, but let's make sure the numbers support that *in real time*, not just in manifestation mode.

This is the moment when you have honest conversations with yourself. Are you offloading stress into your spending? Are you using investments as proof of worth instead of tools for growth? Are you trying to bypass the discomfort of feeling like I'm not good enough?

Because the truth is: you don't need to prove anything. And you definitely don't have to spend your way into worth.

When you lead from your values, stay grounded in your numbers, and choose to pay yourself *while living* within your means, you step into a new kind of leadership. One that's calm, capable, and clear. You stop reacting to pressure, and start responding with vision.

That's what we're building here.

Let's start with how you get paid.

There are two ways entrepreneurs make money from their businesses.

The first is your salary—the amount you pay yourself for the work you do *in* the business. You're the coach, the advisor, the consultant, the doctor, or the artist. You show up and serve your clients. And if you had to hire someone else to do what you do at your level of expertise, what would that cost? That's the baseline. You should be earning at least that.

The second is profit—what's left over after every expense is paid. Rent, software, admin, payroll, your salary, team benefits, all of it. Profit is your reward for being the one who said yes. You held the vision. You took the risk. You worked for free in the early days. You created jobs, delivered value, and built something from nothing.

Profit is your reward for courage. And you deserve it.

As my business grew, first to $1 million, then to $5 million, and beyond, I had to learn how to give myself raises along the way. And honestly? It felt weird at first. Like I needed permission. Even though I was the one taking on the risk and responsibility, I hesitated to increase my salary.

My role had changed. I wasn't just a financial advisor anymore; I was the CEO of a fast-growing company. I was leading, hiring, and building. But for a while, my compensation didn't reflect that shift.

That's a problem.

Because your salary should grow as your business grows. As your responsibilities expand, so should your pay. In the beginning, it's easy to justify paying yourself less. You're investing in the business. You're building something bigger. But if you're always the last to get paid, that disconnect will catch up with you emotionally, energetically, and financially.

At $1 million in revenue, I was only paying myself $50K. I told myself it was strategic, and in some ways, it was. I was reinvesting. Hiring. Fueling growth. My personal lifestyle didn't demand more at the time. But underneath that, I was underpaying myself. Severely. Over time, it chipped away at how I felt about my worth.

Paying yourself consistently is a game-changer. It fosters ease, stability, and momentum. It supports your family. It honors your contribution. And it anchors the belief: *I am worthy of being paid.*

When you establish a steady income for yourself, you show up differently. You lead from a place of abundance instead of survival, and make cleaner decisions. And, you grow with confidence.

You need a personal money system, one that mirrors who you are and where you're headed.

The journey to 8 figures means reshaping your relationship with money at every level. That means letting go of old beliefs, healing past wounds, and confidently standing fully in your worth.

You deserve financial success.

You are worthy of a consistent salary.

You didn't go into business to be broke.

You didn't go into business just to take care of everyone else but yourself.

And yet, we're always the first to go without.

You'll be tempted to pour everything back into the business. To hire more help. To invest in coaching, marketing, and bigger systems. And those are good things. You *should* do them.

But not before you take care of yourself and your family. That comes first.

You need a business money plan, that's separate from your personal financial plan. You don't have to choose between them, you get to have both.

# CHAPTER 8

## HUSTLE MONEY TOOLS

### The Numbers Never Lie, but They Sure Tell a Story

If avoidance is the money mindset you need to shift in Hustle, you're likely filling in the blanks with a story that lets you dodge the numbers. The numbers are the truth, they're your scorecard.

And if that last section felt like too much, too dense, too financial, or too far from where you are, I've been there.

When I first started helping entrepreneurs scale to 8 figures, I naturally attracted other financial advisors. We spoke the same language. There was an ease that the Jamie's of this world could copy and paste the tools I offered because money was already their comfort zone. Sure, their mental glass ceilings around shame, fear and toxic Hustle needed to be shattered, but familiarity with money gave them an edge.

Over time, something changed. I began attracting a new type of entrepreneur—the creative one. That's when I realized I also needed to change. When I'd bring up revenue targets or profit margins, I could see the panic set in like an animal caught in the wild. Or, their eyes would glaze over and they'd glance at the clock probably thinking, *How much longer do I have to do this?* Or, their body would freeze.

This was never because they weren't smart or capable, on the contrary. Numbers seemed like a foreign language, one they weren't invited to learn.

One of my private entrepreneurial clients, Claire, is a brilliant coach with a powerful vision. But when we sat down to map her plan, the moment I mentioned a P&L statement, she folded in on herself. I could see how quickly she wanted to disappear. I realized then that I needed a better way to connect with her and present the numbers in a manner that felt safe, empowering, and even creative.

So, I told a story.

And maybe this story sounds like you. Maybe hearing numbers in a personal context is exactly what unlocks it. Even if you're used to talking about money, there might still be mental glass ceilings that only narrative can break.

Meet Vanessa, an estate planning attorney on a mission to grow and scale her business to $10 million in revenue. Her goal is to cover her personal living expenses while reinvesting as much as possible into expanding her services and amplifying her impact.

Vanessa's current annual business revenue was $850,000 per year. She needs $7,000/month for her personal household expenses. That's $84,000 annually in net income she wants to take home. But here's the thing: $84,000 is net, which means after taxes.

Let's do the math: Assume taxes (federal, state, payroll) take 25% of her paycheck. To take home $84,000, Vanessa needs a gross salary of about $112,000 per year (because $112,000 × 75% = approximately $84,000 after taxes).

That means her business needs to allocate:

- $112,000/year to pay her salary
- Plus employer payroll taxes (about 10%) = ~$11,000
- Her total payroll cost for her business is $123,000.

Let's develop a simple operating plan for her.

Here's Vanessa's basic year plan as it currently stands:

- Revenue: $850,000
- Owner's Salary (gross): $112,000
- Payroll Taxes: $11,000
- Business Expenses (staff, rent, tools, marketing, etc.): $450,000
- Total Annual Expenses: $112,000 (salary) + $11,000 (payroll taxes) + $450,000 (business expenses) = **$573,000**
- Profit (before tax): $850,000 (business revenue) - $573,000 (annual business expenses) = **$277,000**

Now Vanessa has her personal life covered and doesn't need to worry about how she'll pay her bills. She has a stable salary she can depend on, easing many money worries.

Her plan also includes a business profit that she can reinvest or use to pay herself a quarterly owner bonus and cover her estimated taxes. She currently has no other cash needs from the business and wants to build reserves before reaching her goal of bringing on another attorney to help her clients plan for their future.

After establishing her salary, we set a goal of saving two months' expenses (total annual expenses $573,000 ÷ 12 = $47,750 × 2 = $95,500) in business savings as reserves.

This will take her less than a year, based on her current growth rate, to save after paying the estimated taxes on the profit. She decides that is the priority in this financial season for her business.

The way I think about the business owner's salary is that it funds their personal lifestyle. And then the profits are what help the owner build wealth. This might involve reinvesting in the business to increase its value or taking a distribution to grow personal wealth.

As a business owner in the Hustle phase, the most valuable gift you can give yourself is living within your means as your business grows. This means keeping your spending within your salary and not using all your profits. Easier said than done, I understand. As your business succeeds and earns more money, you'll want to spend and enjoy the rewards of your hard work. I've been there myself. It's easy to forget about paying taxes, and I promise you, it's no fun to spend all your profits, file your taxes, and then get hit with a six-figure IRS bill.

Living within your means is important. Overspending is often just self-sabotage in disguise; a pressure response masked as productivity. It's the desire to push forward, to reach the next benchmark, or to offload discomfort with another investment or expense.

That's the toxic Hustle talking.

The need to validate your growth externally, the urgency to scale without pausing for assessment, and the reluctance to accept a smaller salary, for now, even when that's the aligned move. This isn't about limitation. This isn't about shrinking. It's about discernment.

This isn't tightening your spending so that you can't play. It's a dance, one that is entirely based on your *values*. Let them show up as line items when you look at your money. That's the foundation of financial maturity. That's how you build a business that grows with you, not against you.

## Start Here

Now it's your turn. If you're past the startup phase, if your business is bringing in more than $50,000 a year, then this next part is essential and non-negotiable. These are the basic steps, yes, but they are powerful. If you've skipped any of them, *now is the time to fix it,* because we're building a business that can scale to 8 figures and beyond. And it begins with a solid structure and clarity.

If you don't have a business financial plan, start by setting a consistent monthly salary for yourself. Ideally, it should match the market rate for your role in the business. But, if your business can't support that yet, your salary should, at the very least, cover your personal living expenses.

And let me be clear, if you're depositing your business revenue into your personal checking account and your revenue is over $50,000 a year, stop reading. Go open a business bank account immediately. I'm serious.

Commingling personal and business finances is a mistake that will cost you.

Here's why:

- Liability: If you've set up an LLC or Corporation, and you should, then one of the major benefits is legal protection. However, mixing personal and business funds can jeopardize that protection. In court, you could be held personally liable for business debts or lawsuits.

- IRS Audit Risk: Commingling increases your chances of an audit by two to three times. It makes deductions more difficult to prove and raises red flags on your tax return.

- Tax Deductions: If you can't properly document a business expense because you used a personal card or can't prove your intent, you could lose that deduction, which could result in back taxes, penalties, and interest.

- Financial Reporting: Mixing accounts makes it almost impossible to generate accurate reports. You won't know your true profit margin, can't plan for growth, and won't be able to secure loans if needed.

- Perception: If you treat your business like a hobby, others will too. The truth is, you're building something of real value. It deserves its own structure, systems, and separation.

Your business exists to provide for you. And that begins with understanding what you need it to deliver.

Get clear on your minimum monthly amount, the sum your business must pay you to cover your personal expenses. Not what you *hope* to make, but what you *need* to make. This isn't about playing small; it's about building something sustainable.

Here's what I see most often. Entrepreneurs typically fall into one of two patterns when paying themselves.

1. They take whatever's left over at the end of the month.
2. They take too much off the top and starve the business of cash.

Neither is a long-term solution.

If you're in the Hustle phase and looking to grow, whether that means hiring, upgrading systems, or investing in strategy, you need to understand what your business must generate just to meet your personal income needs.

That's where your Basic Operating Plan fits in.

This doesn't need to be a 10-page business plan. You're not pitching to a Venture Capital firm. It's a straightforward, simple overview of your income, recurring expenses, and financial runway.

It gives you answers to key questions:

- What's the monthly break-even number?
- What's left for profit or reinvestment?
- How much can I safely pay myself?

Let me give you a real example from a service-based business doing around $750,000 a year:

# Basic Operating Plan

### Projected Revenue

Monthly revenue: $62,500

Total expected annual revenue: $750,000

### Recurring Monthly Expenses

Office rent & utilities: $2,500

Software/tools/subscriptions: $1,000

Marketing platforms: $1,000

Contractor/team support: $10,000

Business owner's salary: $8,000

Team payroll: $15,000

Professional services (CPA, bookkeeping, legal): $1,500

Misc./operating buffer: $2,000

Total Monthly Expenses: $41,000

Annual Total Expenses: $492,000

**<u>Estimated Net Profit: $258,000 (Approx. 34%)</u>**

That $41,000 of monthly expenses is the break-even point. Anything above that is profit or growth capital. You can use it for savings, reinvestment, distributions, and taxes.

This is why having a basic operating plan matters. It gives you visibility so you can see where to cut costs, where to invest, and which levers to pull if you want to increase profits or scale faster.

Ideally, you'll create this plan every year before January. But if you're doing it for the first time, start now. Then, review it monthly. Are you on track? Are you veering off course? Adjust as needed. The goal isn't perfection. The goal is awareness.

Because what you track improves. And what you track, and report, improves exponentially.

You also need capital reserves in your business. This helps you get through slower seasons without spiraling.

If you have recurring revenue, target saving at least 2 months of expenses in your business account. If your model is more launch-based, you'll need to set aside 3–6 months to carry you between cycles.

No one does this. I didn't do it as well as I wish I could, but, you *have* to do it. Just start where you are and build your buffer.

# CHAPTER 9

# THE RIGHT SUPPORT IN HUSTLE

Hustle means doing a lot by yourself. As your business grows, trusting others to help manage your financial picture becomes not just helpful, but essential. Around $250K in revenue, trade the end-of-year, up-past-midnight scramble on the IRS deadline for a support team. Here's who to hire and what to look for:

### Experienced Bookkeeper

Ideally someone who specializes in your industry or business model. They can provide the following:

- Categorize and reconcile your transactions
- Close out your books each month
- Provide accurate profit and loss, balance sheet and cash flow statements
- Help you stay organized and prepared for tax season - no more scrambling at tax time

Why it matters: Most entrepreneurs at this stage only look at their numbers once a year during tax season. A great bookkeeper provides monthly insights to your actual performance, enabling you to course-correct before it's too late.

## Tax Advisor - Enrolled Agent or CPA Who Works With Business Owners

This isn't your average tax preparer. Find one who works with entrepreneurs and will talk in a way you understand. They should offer the following:

- Proactively help you minimize taxes (not just file them)
- Provide advice on entity structure, owner compensation, and deductions
- Help you plan for estimated taxes to avoid surprises
- Partner with your bookkeeper for a seamless year-end close

Why it matters: Tax is one of your biggest expenses. The right strategy can save you tens of thousands each year.

**Business Consultant or Strategist:** - Around $650,000 to $1,000,000 in revenue and nearing five team members, near the end of Hustle or at the start of Surrender stage, a consultant and a guide can help you understand not just your numbers but also the strategy of *HOW* to build your business. And, let me just say, this is my passion. I love helping my private entrepreneurial clients move through this stage, and that love is what inspired this book.

This is someone who:

- Can help you rise above the daily noise and become a strategist for your next level

- Redesign your business to operate independently of your constant involvement by creating structure, systems, and organization within your team

- Gain financial clarity with custom dashboards, forecasts, and tax-smart cash flow, so you know exactly where you stand and how to move forward

- Be your thought partner by helping you clearly define your role and hold you accountable for staying focused

- Help implement scalable systems for offers, client journey, and team accountability that drive outcomes, profit, and predictable growth

Why it matters: It's hard to read the label when you're inside the jar. Having someone who knows where you want to go, guides you through the next level of business, and holds you accountable as you transition from Hustle to Surrender is the best investment you will make.

Not all professionals are created equal. I believe the past experience of your hired support is very important. Ask questions, get to know them, see if you feel intimidated or comfortable with them. You want to be able to ask for help when you need it without feeling stupid, guilty, or ashamed of your choices. They are there to serve you.

## What You Don't Want to (or Maybe Can't Even) Think About

Most readers of this book are somewhere in Hustle or Surrender, maybe even knocking on the door of Harmony. Without a doubt, Hustle and Surrender are the most challenging seasons of building a business. You are constructing an airplane mid-flight, crossing your fingers that the duct tape on the wings holds steady when turbulence hits. Talking about giving generously can feel impossible to hear over the clanging metal of your sweet air bus.

I get it. You are focused, likely worried, about making rent, covering payroll, and paying overhead expenses. The idea of giving to others might seem out of reach when you're still putting the oxygen mask on yourself.

And yet, this is the time.

I often introduce expanded giving plans in the season of Surrender, when business owners face a six-figure tax bill and feel the weight of their success pressing in. But the roots of generosity can and should be planted earlier. Even in Hustle.

I've seen entrepreneurs create massive philanthropic change simply because they are motivated by tax benefits. What happens next, though, is where the real magic begins. The joy, connection, and elation of giving generously rewire their thinking the moment they see and feel the impact. And once someone begins giving, it rarely stops with a single act. It becomes a way of being.

If "way of being" feels like too much right now, that's okay. It's hard to give when you're in Hustle. But I want you to start thinking about it. In Hustle, giving doesn't always mean writing checks. It could mean mentoring, volunteering your time on a non-profit board, or taking on a pro bono client who touches your heart. Whatever it is, find it, and start now.

## HUSTLE CHECKLIST:

1. **Hustle Mindset – Lead with fire.**
   Let your passion drive the momentum. This is the season for building, stretching, and going all in.

2. **Personal Values – Anchor yourself to what truly matters.**
   Hustle without alignment leads to burnout and can be toxic. Your values are the filter. Let them guide every decision.

3. **90-Day Season – Build with boundaries.**
   Build in seasons. Know what each one is for, and what it's not.

4. **Money Mindset – Face the money.**
   Avoiding your numbers will cost you. Face them. Know them. Let them show you what's real and what's possible.

5. **Financial Separation – Draw the line.**
   Your business and personal finances must live in separate lanes. No exceptions.

6. **Operating Plan – Keep it simple.**
   A clear blueprint for revenue, expenses, and profit.

7. **Financial Reports – Know your numbers.**
   You don't need to run your P&L daily, but you better know what it is. In Hustle, financials are often buried in email, shoeboxes, or forgotten altogether. That stops now.

8. **Legal Foundation – Be legit.**
   LLC or corporation established, dedicated business accounts, and proper accounting software.

9.  **Consistent Pay – Pay yourself intentionally.**
    You are on a salary, not an owner's draw. Consistency is the key here.

10. **Financial Team – Bring in support.**
    A bookkeeper, a tax advisor; people who speak numbers and bring order.

# PART TWO: SURRENDER

## The Surrender Process

# CHAPTER 10

# CONGRATULATIONS, YOU'RE ON THE WAY TO FIRING YOURSELF!

Jamie attracted an investor for his business, but couldn't sell it. He was trying to take chips off the table from his $100-million-plus business. He had poured everything into it and millions in annual revenue, a mile-long client list, a product people loved, and yet, after all the months of courting the right private equity group, which fueled Jamie's heart, no one invested. He was stunned.

I wasn't. I knew why the second I saw his Customer Relationship Management (CRM) platform.

We were sitting in a conference room at the Ritz-Carlton in Orlando. Jamie had pulled up his CRM to show off a new integration of his dashboard highlighting all of his business metrics. It was a version of my Freedom Dashboard™, a top sheet, on steroids, and honestly, it was stunning. The kind of system founders dream of building and investors love to see. I told him it was *business sexy*. I pulled out my camera, already snapping shots and asked, "Can I take a picture of this? It's incredible?" I instantly sent it to my team's Slack channel so we could build something just as astonishing as this was.

And it was. Until I asked, "Who else has access?" He simply said. "No one." I blinked and in my shock of surprise I might have raised my voice by saying, "I'm sorry... What?"

Across the room, one of our mutual friends looked over with interest, "Julia, what are you doing?"

"Giving him shit," I said, not missing a beat.

Yes, Jamie could have sold his business or brought in an investor, but not for what it could truly be worth. That was the blind spot he couldn't see, yet it was so obvious to me. He was never going to realize the full value of his company because this self-made man had, in the end, made himself the problem. Private equity firms have a name for this: *key man risk*. When too much of the business relies on one person, it's a liability. Jamie didn't see it that way. He called it *protection*.

But I called it what it really was: "Jamie, *you* are the problem."

You can be making tens of millions of dollars a year and still be unbuyable. You can have the revenue, the clients, and the team, but if everything relies on you, then the business isn't the asset. *You* are. And no one wants to buy a business they can't run without the founder glued to the seat.

It doesn't matter what you call it—protection, control, perfectionism—at some point, you have to let it go. You have to shift from being in control to being in charge. From doing everything yourself to leading it effectively.

Eventually, Jamie began to trust his very capable COO, hired a president, and stepped way back. He put the pieces into that place that would make him more valuable for a private equity firm to invest in his business. And a year later, it was to the tune of $50 million dollars more. That's how well this works.

"Congratulations," I told him, "you just fired yourself!"

He laughed at the comment, "Julia, no one's ever said that to me before."

It didn't take Jamie long to course-correct. I think seeing that the pain of his company, his baby, valued below its true worth prompted deep reflection, which led him to dramatically change his business structure.

Regardless of how someone gets there, the key move is firing yourself. Yet, most businesses don't succeed. Not because their product or service isn't good, but because investors, private equity partners, or buyers don't believe the business can scale without the founder at the center of everything.

"Congratulations, you fired yourself!" is the sentence every founder eventually needs to hear and the lesson every entrepreneur must learn. I wish it would have been that easy for me, Surrendering. But just like Jamie, I had to learn it the hard way. He learned it when his company was undervalued.

I had to learn it in a hospital.

# CHAPTER 11

# THE SURRENDER MINDSET

## The Call of Freedom

The light never changed in the ICU. It was just a cold, sterile glare that stood watch as I sat by Katelyn's bed, praying she would recover from the head-on collision that left her with internal bleeding, broken ribs, a punctured lung, and a lacerated spleen. Days were spent watching the monitors shift, listening to them beep in the hopes that she was healing and wouldn't need surgery. As a parent, there is no pain greater than watching your child suffer and feeling powerless to stop it. Its agony knows no equal.

During that time, nothing else mattered; my focus was solely on my daughter's recovery. Yet, even there, even in that most important space of healing, my business kept tugging at me. I had built a machine that could not run without me. As much as I resented that truth, I had to own it.

I was the one who made myself indispensable. I was the one addicted to being needed. I had become the bottleneck in my own life.

Katelyn's accident didn't just wake me up to the fragility of life, it shattered the illusion I had been clinging to for years. I thought I was building a business for freedom. But when it truly mattered, I wasn't free at all.

A core value for every entrepreneur I've ever worked with is this: freedom. It's the reason we do what we do. We want freedom in all areas of life: time, creativity, leadership, financial independence, work with who we want to work with, and spending life with those we love most.

And honestly, when I started my business, it was what I wanted more than anything.

Freedom became my mantra. It was my word of the year. It was my screensaver. It was my password. I even named my company, Financial Freedom Wealth Management as an homage to my personal desire for freedom.

Building my business, working *in* it, and working *on* it made me feel alive. It made me feel important. I could measure my worth in growth, momentum, and money. I was helping people. I was making things happen.

I imagined that freedom would arrive somehow. Maybe it would show up at my office door, knocking with flowers, champagne, and the sense of self-worth I desperately longed for. So, I kept chasing freedom. Maybe it would come after the next milestone, the next hire, if I hit the 8-figure mark, if I made the Forbes list, if I fixed the systems, or if I proved I could do it all.

But it doesn't work that way. The Hustle got me here, but it wasn't going to get me to where I really wanted to go because I was completely at the end of my limits. There were no more hours in the day, no more meals I could skip, and no more ways I could stretch myself. Unbeknownst to me, I was actually trapped in the Entrepreneurial Sprial™ — a years-long painful plateau.

Katelyn's accident shattered my mental glass ceiling with such force that it changed everything: a true "before and after" event.

To step into ultimate freedom, you must be willing to see things differently.

Have you ever been fired from a job? It doesn't feel good, nobody wants to be fired. And I am asking you to do that to yourself because firing yourself *is* the Surrender.

It is the essential realization required of you. It's a painful repetition because the plateaus of any business will always, *yes always*, reflect a need to mentally reinvent yourself by letting go of jobs that no longer support the long-term health of the business. Surrender is the most emotionally charged part of the entrepreneurial journey, the heart of this book and the hardest part for me to write because it is something that I as an entrepreneur have to do over and over. Surrender is not weakness, it's the wisdom to let go of control.

It's about accepting help, and architecting something entirely different. Allowing your team to execute without you, hiring differently, delegating decisively by having others own outcomes rather than tasks, and implementing systems that scale without you. Sometimes it's a new person. Sometimes it's a new platform.

But always, it's a new way of thinking so that you can create a new way of being. You start trusting your team because you hired well. You begin trusting your intuition, because you cast the vision. You stop doing everything and instead focus on leading it.

This is a cycle that remains consistent because it's uncomfortable and just happens to be non-negotiable for growth.

It ain't easy, trust me.

And if you ignore the signs long enough, they start to show up in your schedule, your bottom line, and in your body.

## If You Don't Fire Yourself, Your Body Will

You are not your business.

I know it doesn't feel that way when you've built it from the ground up, when it's your vision, your name, and your reputation, it can feel impossible to separate the two. Firing yourself doesn't just threaten your systems; it threatens your sense of being, which is incredibly frightening.

My private entrepreneurial client, Claire, who I mentioned earlier, is a powerhouse, and this year, her body gave her the wake-up call of a lifetime.

She had 7 full-on grand mal seizures in a short period of time. If you're unfamiliar, a typical seizure is a sudden electrical burst in the brain that might appear as a blank stare, a moment of disconnection, or a few seconds of twitching. But a grand mal seizure is entirely different. It hijacks the whole body. Muscles lock up followed by convulsions. They are violent, uncontrollable, and absolutely terrifying.

The doctors searched for answers, but the truth was deeper than a medical diagnosis. Her body was loudly waving the white flag. It was saying, *enough*.

After the first grand mal seizure, she pulled back slightly, mainly out of fear. She delegated some responsibilities, canceled a few meetings, and decided to "take it easy." But as soon as she started feeling better, her old patterns returned immediately. She took everything back onto her plate and pushed her barely recovered body to keep up. In her mind, she didn't want to burden her team, you know, the team she had hired to handle her business duties. Showing weakness, incapability, or unreliability wasn't something Claire was willing to reveal to others, let alone herself. So, she did what most of us have done in that situation: she controlled. Because sometimes, control can feel easier than trust.

And then it happened again. Another grand mal seizure.

We often talk about burnout like it's a mindset issue, which it can be. But sometimes, it's rather literal. If you keep holding the business on your back because you're afraid to let go, eventually your body will make the decision for you.

As entrepreneurs and founders, it can sometimes be challenging to wrap your very tired thoughts around the idea that firing yourself isn't about laziness. It's a structural and strategic business move—one that's required if you want to scale, grow, and hopefully sell one day. Surrendering isn't about checking out or losing control. It's about reclaiming your leadership without having to white-knuckle your way through every email, decision, and crisis that comes your way.

Claire's body told her what her mind refused to see: Surrender isn't failure. It's the only way forward.

## The Trifecta of Control

Between Jamie, Claire, and me, there was an invisible triangle of control that formed: three different stories, one shared pattern. We Diet-Coked, white-knuckled, overworked, and over-functioned our way through success until each of us hit our own wall, shaped by the limits of our mental glass ceilings. Control wasn't just a habit; it had become our identity.

We each came to Surrendering, and firing ourselves, through the companies we built, but we each took different paths to get there. Jamie found it through trusting his team. I had to unravel the identity I had constructed around being needed. Claire's body forced her to stop.

Three founders. Three breaking points. One universal truth: if you don't surrender control, something else will take it from you.

Surrender may not seem easy, but it's the only one that leads to true freedom.

# CHAPTER 12

# SURRENDER TOOLS

## Magic Wand 2.0

Back in Hustle, you cast a vision with the first magic wand, the one that imagined *your* dream life. Maybe it looked like unadulterated time to create and work in the business you founded. Maybe it looked like the flexibility to travel the world spending your first 90-day season in Buenos Aires, and the next 90-day season in Auckland. Or maybe it looked like the simplistic freedom of long walks with a partner, an extended dinner with inspiring clients, the zero-inbox kind of days. That vision was personal.

But this time, it's no longer about you.

This one is about business. What it could become if you let it?

Hopefully by now, you've begun loosening your grip on all the hats you wear. Or at the very least, you've started to see that you're wearing too many. And once you're no longer the one holding everything together, you're finally free to ask:

*What could this business become without me at the center of everything?*

This is where you stop driving the bus, hire someone to steer, and start charting the course.

This is one of the most overlooked exercises in the entrepreneur's journey who had not scaled. Not because founders don't dream big, but because their dreams stay trapped in their heads with a map to places only they can see. It looks like ideas that float around in voice notes, or scribbled in margins, or half-mentioned to a peer who gets it, but rarely does this dream make it into a playbook a team can follow.

And if your team can't see it, they can't build it.

Now's the time to put that vision somewhere outside of your mind, even if it's messy, half-baked, or feels like a child with a box of crayons could do better. Your team doesn't need perfection. They need direction. Your business can't fully align with a vision that only exists *in* your head.

Let's make it real.

Let's cast your vision with the upgraded version of your magic wand, the one where the business grows up, expands outward, and surpasses even you.

## The Magic Wand Exercise - Business Edition

**Step 1: Ask yourself these questions**

- If I waved a magic wand, what would your business look like three, five and ten years from now?
- Who would it serve and how?
- What would you be known for in the market or in the world?

- What kind of results, transformation, or experience would define your business?
- What type of team would be needed to deliver on that promise?
- What would your role *have to* look to become that future business? What would you no longer be doing?
- What kind of Legacy would this business leave behind, beyond profit?

This is just a draft where you are the original author, feel free to revise it any time. So grab a pen, make a voice note, or take yourself on what I like to call a *Possibility Walk*: thirty minutes where you unplug from the to-do list and let yourself dream a little. (This is usually where I get my best downloads, by the way. Movement unlocks vision.)

## STEP 2: Express it

Once you have a vision, the next step is to start to say it out loud to the people who matter and the ones you trust—your team, your partners, your besties—the people helping you build. This isn't always a person with a pulse on markets. But the people you turn to here are the ones who deserve and have earned the right to share in your story. Choose wisely.

It doesn't need to be perfect. Some of my best ideas for my business started as scribbles on a legal pad or voice notes I'd listen to later and laugh at. But it doesn't matter how it sounds. The important thing is that it's out in the open.

Because if the vision only lives in your mind, your team can't align with it. The moment you make it visible, even as just a draft, is the moment you stop holding the future alone.

And that's when you know you're leading it.

## Goldilocks

Early in my business, all I wanted was to be the best financial advisor I could be. I loved it. I obsessed over it. I spent thousands of hours, and just as many dollars, mastering my craft. I got certified, coached, and mentored. I built relationships one meeting at a time, even making house calls to the middle of nowhere, rural Oregon. I earned trust by taking late-night calls and going above and beyond. I delivered results. That was the entire game to me: Be great at what you do, and you'll build something that lasts.

And I did. Forbes and Barron's now say so, too.

But as the business grew into multiple 7 figures, I had to face a hard truth; being a great advisor wasn't enough anymore. I had to choose. Was I going to stay in the weeds, or step into a role where the business could grow beyond me, make a greater impact, and help more clients pursue financial independence than I ever could on my own?

Did I want to keep running the numbers, managing the team, touching every file, holding every thread?

Or did I want to lead from the seat no one else could fill?

For a long time, I resisted it. I needed to find the right fit, for me, my team, and the business. I liked being involved in daily operations. I liked being known by all my clients. I liked being the one everyone came to. I was good at it, and it felt great to be needed. But deep down, I knew I couldn't be the CFO, COO, and CEO all at once.

So, I chose.

I chose to become the CEO. And more than that, I embraced being the visionary of my company. I'm not leading the operations of the business, I am the one casting the bigger picture and protecting the future direction of the business.

My wealth management firm's vision today is simple:

*To be the nation's most caring financial advisory team guiding you, your loved ones, and your Legacy toward lasting financial independence and a life of fulfillment.*

Neither choice, CFO, COO, or CEO, is right or wrong. But as the business owner, I had to redefine my role to evolve with the business.

These titles can get yoked to your identity, and shedding them creates a kind of weird state of entrepreneurial limbo; a space where you're no longer in the old role, but not yet grounded in the new one. You have to live through and learn to dance in that in-between tension. Which can be, and I speak from experience here, very uncomfortable.

If you're early in your entrepreneurial journey, you may not have reached your initial vision yet, and that's okay. This book will guide you to it. And when you do reach it, be prepared for it to shift. You'll change, too. And that's the best part of being an entrepreneur!

Because you don't grow into the next version of your business by holding on to the one that got you here.

## Values - But This Time It's Business.

In our old building, my office was front and center on the first floor. I was in the thick of everything. Clients would wander in unannounced, and I could hear every conversation around me. One teammate might be chatting about the latest cliffhanger on a true crime docuseries, another sharing a funny story about their kid's breakfast meltdown, someone else passing along a review of the gym that just opened across the street. But without a doubt, the biggest distractions were always the client calls. I'd only catch one side of the conversation and then jump in midstream like a well-meaning but over-eager coach shouting plays from the sideline. My intentions were good, but my impact was... less than helpful.

Not only did I exhaust myself by joining every conversation where I believe I could contribute, I unintentionally gave my team the impression that they weren't capable. And while I cringe at this now, I know our clients also sensed that dynamic.

In 2017, when we built our new office, I had enough self-awareness, and enough Surrender in my system, to know I needed to make a move. Literally. I relocated upstairs into what I now call The Nest—a spacious, light-filled corner office tucked into the quietest part of the building. This move was partly strategic, but fully infused with Surrender energy. I had to stop micromanaging and start trusting my team. I had to believe that if something truly needed my attention, whether a client concern or an operational hiccup, it would find its way to me.

And while my team was always kind, that's the kind of people I hire, I'm sure they all breathed a quiet sigh of relief when I moved into The Nest.

When I began to fire myself, pulling back from unnecessary conversations and leading with trust, I needed to know the business could stand on its own. I needed to know the soul of what I'd built wouldn't vanish the moment I stepped back. That's when I guided my team through defining our business values.

Your personal values shape who you are. Your business values shape how your company operates. While personal values evolve as you move through different seasons of life, your business values are the stabilizing force that keeps your culture strong.

When I created this methodology, we had about eight team members, and it was the year after we had doubled our revenue. We were growing fast. I was actively letting go of responsibilities, and the business needed a clear identity of its own.

We gathered in the conference room. Behind each team member's chair, I hung one of those giant sticky Post-its and grabbed a handful of colorful Sharpies. One by one, we took turns naming each person's best qualities. We shared not only what we admired but also what we'd seen when no one was looking. We recalled glowing client feedback and quiet moments, like when someone stayed late to help or gave a teammate a ride home. I stood behind each person and captured their qualities as fast as I could. Words came pouring out. I scribbled furiously as I heard "integrity," "respect," "delight," "team player," "calm under pressure," "solution-focused." I wrote it all down.

From that raw data, we stepped back and looked at the vibrant words scattered across the room, filling those oversized pages around the conference table. This was our compass. This was who we were, not just me, the founder. These words were a mirror, reflecting the best of us and how we wanted to move through the world. From that session, we uncovered our core values. They are:

- Treat all people with respect
- Never compromise our integrity
- Delight our Clients
- Embrace our team culture

Those words have guided us ever since. We hire by them. We lead by them. We recognize and reward by them. They are alive in our business, not just some platitudes scribbled on a wall. They've helped us scale with consistency, even as we've added locations, team members, and service lines.

When your business has clearly defined values, it no longer relies on you to keep the culture intact. The values do the heavy lifting because you have done enough. They become the standard everyone can live up to, and the container that holds everything together.

Now it's your turn.

## Discover Your Business Core Values

**Instructions:** You can follow my lead, do the following or get creative and make it your own.

1. Look at your rockstar team members. Who are the top 3–5 people in your company you'd clone if you could? What do they consistently do or believe that makes them great?

2. Be specific. What do these people do? Do they go above and beyond? Solve problems quickly? Show up with kindness? Speak the truth? Take ownership?

3. Find the themes. Group similar traits together and give them a short, memorable name (e.g., Own It, Speak Love, Do What's Right, Be Better Every Day).

4. Define 3-6 business core values clearly. Write a one-sentence definition for each value that includes what it looks like in action. (e.g., We Before Me ~ We work as a team, support each other, and win together. Own it ~ We take full responsibility for results, no blame, no excuses.)

**Top Business Core Values:**
1.
2.
3.
4.
5.

Having defined core values will help you fire yourself and hire people who are genuinely excited by and aligned with them. And if someone isn't, their behavior will make it obvious. In most cases, they'll opt out before you have to make the tough call.

Values also give your executive team a clear framework for leadership. They allow you to coach and mentor without making it personal. It's no longer about one person's opinion; it's about the standard the entire team has agreed to uphold.

Defined, stated core values are how you step out of the day-to-day and trust that what you've built will continue to grow and thrive without you at the center.

# CHAPTER 13

# THE SURRENDER AUDIT

I met Jason and Angel on a cold November morning in 2010. My company didn't yet have an office in the Willamette Valley, so I invited them to meet me at a local bakery. And yes, I still have the notes from that day, scribbled across a beat-up note pad, marked with numbers, a few doodles, and the unmistakable drive of an entrepreneur moving from Hustle to Surrender without realizing it. At the top of the page, in bold letters, it read *Carlson Financial Group*. Four years later, I would remove my name from the company altogether, renaming it *Financial Freedom Wealth Management Group*. That decision marked something deeper than a rebrand, it was the symbolic firing of myself from the firm that bore my name.

Inside the bakery, it was warm but packed. I remember scanning the tables, finding a corner where we could speak quietly because we were talking about money—their money. And though I didn't know it at the time, I wasn't just gaining two clients that day. It was the beginning of a relationship that would change everything about how I built my business.

Fast-forward to 2013. Angel and I were sitting in a McDonald's playground, the kind with sticky tables and the sound of toddlers echoing off plastic slides. Of all places to experience a seismic shift in the trajectory of my business, I would never have guessed it would happen there.

I wanted to hire Jason.

I could see it. I knew he had the mindset, skill set, and exact energy I was looking for. But Angel wasn't sure. Not about him, about me. Who was this woman? Could she trust me? Even though I had been managing her money for the better part of three years, she was skeptical. I was asking her to believe in a dream that hadn't fully materialized yet. I was asking her to leap.

So, I sold her on the vision.

I told her we were building something big. That Jason was going to make six figures. That if she trusted the process, if she stayed in it with me, we'd create something extraordinary. And I meant it.

But the Surrender process takes as long as it takes.

He didn't join right away and I didn't rush the timeline. Instead, I stayed focused on my 90-day season, what I could do, build, and align in that window to create the kind of business that could actually support someone earning a solid six-figure salary. That was my job in the Hustle to Surrender transition: laying the foundation for the next level of leadership.

Eventually, Jason joined the team. First as an advisor and then in larger roles within the company. But it was his self-leadership, his ability to own outcomes by using strategic and critical thinking to solve problems that arose, that became an invaluable asset. Today, he's my right hand, my #2; an integral part of any successful business who is compensated with a strong 6-figure salary, carries the title of President and is a partner in the company.

Back then, if you asked me whether I would ever have a partner, I would have said *absolutely not*. I was the founder, I was the only one who could do it all the right way.

But Jason showed me what was possible when you let someone else carry the vision with you, alongside you. He didn't just help me build the business; he made it stronger than I ever could have on my own. If you want to go fast, go alone. If you want to go far, go together.

This is the hallmark of Surrender.

## Structure That Scales - Structure Isn't Sexy. Until it is.

My husband, Chris, owns a construction company that builds people's dream homes on the Oregon coast—cliffside mansions with floor-to-ceiling windows that open to the Pacific, cedar-lined A-frames, and cozy cottages tucked away on private land. However, when a client wants a renovation, they often hit a snag: the foundation is unstable. The house may not be anchored properly or the bedrock is sagging into the clay around it. The client's vision simply can't be supported. In those cases, the only real option is a full rebuild tearing down the existing structure, preparing the land, laying a proper foundation, and then building the home they truly want.

This conversation is less than fun to deliver to a client, but imperative for the long-term health of their home. They can dream up the most exquisite design: gleaming hardwood floors that beg for bare-foot love, a deck made for summer gatherings, the perfect light fixtures casting a golden glow. But if the soil underneath is slowly eroding, no chandelier can outshine a sinking house.

In Hustle, there is no structure, there is no time to look at curtains or choose paint colors. You're just trying to throw up some walls and a roof hoping the elements don't take you out. There's only chaos with you at the center of it all. But Surrender marks the start of something different.

If you dream of building something bigger than yourself, you've most likely felt the weight of that growth. The more success you achieve, the heavier it can become—more decisions, more people, more moving parts. And if you're still in every room, still answering every question, still approving every detail, that's not leadership. That's just another version of Hustle, and not what this is about.

Structure is the way out. It isn't sexy until it works, but when it does, it's the most attractive thing you've ever seen, your dream home on solid ground, built to last.

The Hustle Audit™ underscores where your time and energy are really going. The Surrender Audit highlights what you're still gripping; what needs to be released, ready or not. Seeing your business laid out visually helps you see where you're still holding on, and what can be delegated. That's why I created the WOW (Who Owns What) Outcomes Chart™. It's the exact system I used to scale to 8 figures, and it's the same one I now use to guide my 7-figure entrepreneurs into the land of 8 figures and beyond.

## WOW Outcomes Chart™ (Who Owns What)

I'm not often in Vegas, but if I were to place a sizable bet on whether you, the founder, are doing most, if not all, of the jobs in your company, I'd cash in big.

There's real power in naming your roles, acknowledging the capacity you've been holding, and validating the work you're already doing.

When I map my private entrepreneurial clients' businesses, that ah-ha moment often brings both emotional and structural chaos. I hear it all the time: "I had no idea I was owning every part of this business." But that's where the magic begins.

The next step goes beyond the Hustle Audit™. It's a deeper exercise I call *Map the Machine*—a Venn diagram of everything you're doing as the founder. It shows, in one clear picture, exactly where your time, energy, and focus are going, and where they need to shift next.

About a month ago, I sat with one of my private entrepreneurial clients as we mapped her current state of business onto her Venn diagram (one similar to the example below). I watched her expression shift from shock to curiosity, and then to clarity. From that grounded place of awareness, she could finally see the weight she'd been carrying by trying to fulfill every need and role of the business herself. It was a profound moment and one I had the privilege to witness. It was the beginning of something new. That realization gave her the freedom to fire herself from the roles that were draining her most valuable resource: her energy.

## CURRENT STATE OF BUSINESS

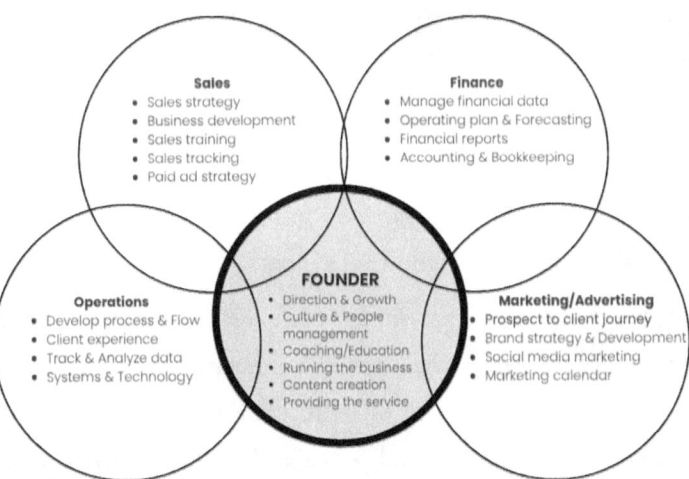

Using the above example, where are you still owning outcomes that are not yours to have? Or ones that drain your energy, time and focus? This is not about what's right or wrong. This is data for you, the business owner. I often see confusion here because the business grew fast, you hired team members without clearly defined roles because you needed help with everything and everyone just figured it out. That's normal. But now, it's time to be intentional.

*If I had to step away for 90 days, what would break?*

Wherever the answer is *me*, that's your bottleneck. That's where we start.

You're not just looking at what you do. You're deciding what you're done doing.

Start with the things that drain you. Those roles or tasks that zap your energy (refer to your The Hustle Audit™). Your ability to scale is directly proportional to how energized you feel. If you don't feel excited, those items are your first exits. And, you know what to say when you exit those roles, right?

When you can see where you need to fire yourself, you can sketch out your ideal structure chart. Not the one we just created, but the one with the new foundation—the one you need.

At the top: You.

Next: You are ultimately going to have a second in command, a #2 that will be the first in control while you remain in charge. You may not have this person right now and that's okay.

Beneath that, core departments with clear roles and responsibility. You may not have the "who" but the job and its outcomes must be defined. You will not need to hire everyone today, in fact, I wouldn't recommend it. But you do need to see and understand the structure so you can grow into it. You can still be in every box as you are growing. When you are ready to hand off the box, you are not just giving the tasks *but rather the responsibility of ownership of that position to the appropriate hire.*

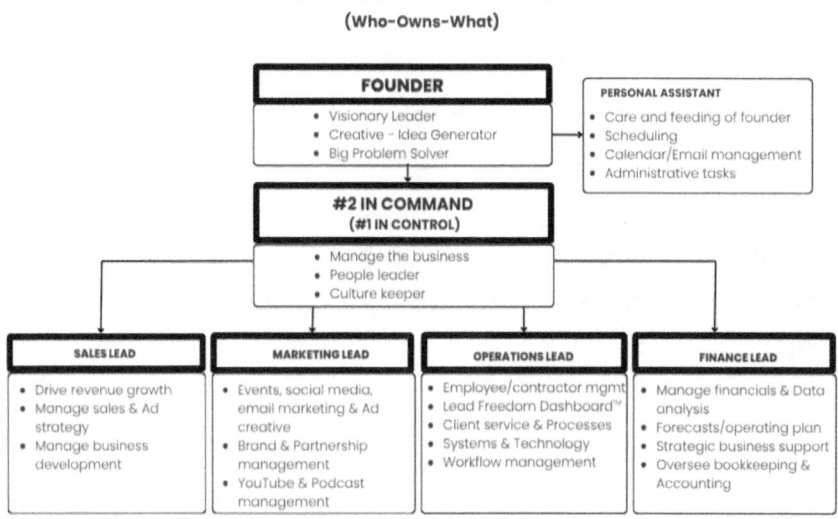

Surrender isn't blind. You're not just handing over the reins; you're building the structure and systems that will allow you to trust and verify. It's not an overnight process, but it's the one that matters most at this stage. Investing in people, systems, and structure now will pay off exponentially down the road. This is the unglamorous work that, when done right, becomes incredibly attractive.

## Hiring a #2

Hiring a real number two changes everything. But it also requires you to change.

Because a number two isn't a task-taker, or a virtual assistant with an overwhelming to-do list. Nor are they someone who needs hand-holding. A true number two *owns outcomes.* I call them essential intrapreneurs; people who think and act like entrepreneurs inside your business. They are self-led, drive results, and solve problems correctly before you even see them. They take things off your plate, not because you asked, but because they know it's theirs now.

And that can be... confronting. It was for me.

A good number two will challenge you. They'll question your decisions. They'll ask, "Why are we doing it this way?" or "Is this the best use of your time?" If you're used to being the smartest person in the room, or the one in control of everything (*clears throat*), that can feel like a threat.

Which, of course, is not a threat; it's the answer to scaling your business to 8 figures and beyond.

The first time I hired my number two, I wasn't totally ready. Most entrepreneurs that I've taught this process to aren't either. It takes time to actually find a #2, but it also takes time to internally process the stage of the spiral you might find yourself in. The entrepreneur needs to reflect when they hit those plateaus that inevitably arise.

Internal dialogue might sound like:

> *"I thought I gave up the wheel, but I'm still gripping it."*
> *"Their feedback feels like an attack, even though they're right."*
> *"If they're doing the job I used to do, what's mine now?"*

When you hire correctly, the #2 will stretch and teach you in unexpected ways that you weren't ready for, and the lessons come fast and quick. But if there is one thing I've learned on my own journey and helping guide others, it's that you don't need someone who cares the same way you do. You need someone who cares about the *right* things. And only you as the business owner can decide what those things might be.

Everything else? Let it go.

Finding the right person might take a few tries, that's normal. It's a part of the game you play when you step into the larger-than-life arena called "Business - Let's Scale to 8 Figures and Beyond!" But when you get it right, you'll wonder how you ever ran your business without them. Truthfully, you can't. The #2 is one of the most pivotal hires in your business and personal life. And if from time to time, they trigger you a little... or a lot? Good. That means they're strong where you're not. Which was the whole point to begin with.

## How to Hire

Hiring isn't about filling a seat. If that were the goal, it would be simple. But every new person you bring into your company has the potential to shift the energy of your culture, your momentum, and your results. Hiring someone who isn't aligned can cost far more than just their salary. It can slow the team down, frustrate your high performers, and chip away at the trust you've worked hard to build.

Hiring takes time and money, whether you're opening a new role or replacing someone. And you're not hiring a replica; you're hiring for what's next. Sometimes the person who got you from point A to point B isn't the same person who will take you through the rest of the alphabet.

That's why hiring well matters.

It starts with culture. Ken Blanchard said it best; culture eats strategy for breakfast. If the culture isn't healthy, it's hard to attract the right people. Culture sets the tone for how your team performs and how your clients feel. It influences everything. I talk more about building a values-driven culture in Harmony, but here's the key. Culture isn't something that just happens. You choose it. You live it. You protect it. And when it's strong, hiring becomes a whole lot easier.

I fired myself from hiring pretty early in my Surrender journey. I had a serious flaw in hiring. I liked everyone. I always saw their potential. My bestie calls me "The Maximizer." It's true. I know how to draw out people's strengths. That is, if they are willing, hence my flaw. This has bitten me in the butt more times than I can count and, maybe like me, you leading the hiring process may not be the highest value add to your business. Firing yourself isn't just allowing you to be in your highest and most skilled positions, it's protective in nature by keeping you out of the roles that you have no business playing. The creative bandwidth I have poured into my business by actively removing myself from hiring outcomes is immeasurable. Now, I have no idea of how to post a job listing and I shouldn't know.

There are going to be a lot of swings and misses in your hiring process—I know this firsthand. During my Surrender stage, I didn't have an HR person. My #2 carried the weight of the hiring process alongside the potential new hire's future manager. I knew enough about myself to recognize that hiring wasn't my strength, but I also knew we needed people, and fast.

Without the right systems, we learned everything through trial and error. The number of lessons from our early hiring attempts could fill an entire book. I did what I could with the skills I had, piecing together a patchwork process that kept us moving forward. Still, I wish I'd had the clarity and structure I'm sharing here.

## What Seat Are We Filling?

Now that the members of my executive team run this aspect of our business, it's still crafted from the vision I set as a CEO. So before we ever post a position, we get clear on what we're hiring for. We don't just list tasks. We think about the gap we need to fill, how this role will impact the business, and what kind of person would thrive in our environment. If I knew to ask these questions, I would have:

- What outcome or role are we trying to fill?
- What specific abilities are we looking for?
- How will those abilities move the company forward?
- Is this something we need a full-time person for, or could we outsource it?
- Are we looking for someone seasoned, or can we train and coach them?
- What will this role cost based on market research?
- What's our budget for the role?
- How will this hire free up our time and others on the team?
- Is this the right time to hire?

Once those pieces are in place, then we write the posting. We want it to reflect who we are. We want the right person to read it and feel like we're speaking directly to them. So we give it some life. We add the energy and tone of our culture. We don't sugarcoat anything. We want someone to know exactly what they're walking into. That's how we build trust from the very beginning.

Once the post is live, engage. Even though your slack is blowing up on a separate business issue, respond quickly, communicate clearly, and treat every candidate like they matter. Because they do. Whether they're the right fit or not, they're giving us their time and attention.

We build our questions around culture, values, and impact. Right now, as you are looking to hire, your team and business culture will be formed *as you hire*. It's the same "building the airplane midflight" metaphor in Hustle, and that's okay. There's more about creating and solidifying your team culture in Harmony, but for now, you can use this as a guideline for hiring. Some are specific to the role, some are just fun. These questions are designed to help you get to the heart of who a person is, how they communicate, and whether they'll thrive in your environment.

A few of our favorites:

- What qualities make you a team player?
  (Tied to our "Embrace our Team Culture" value.)

- If you strongly disagreed with a decision from leadership, how would you respond?
  (This tests our "Treat Everyone with Respect" value.)

- Tell me about a time you witnessed non-integrity. What did you do?
  (Aligned with our "Never compromise our Integrity" value.)

- What's your favorite type of donut?
  (Culture isn't just about performance, it's about personality.)

- What do you love doing outside of work?
  (We want whole humans, not just résumés.)

After each round, our team debriefs. We look for alignment, gaps, and concerns. We ask: Does this person raise the bar? Will they elevate the team? Will they grow with us?

If the answer is no, even if I personally love them, we pass. During my Surrender stage, we could hire people in a couple weeks, but now, it usually takes a month, sometimes longer. We keep it efficient, but we never rush it.

Hiring right isn't just good for the company, it's good for the culture. Because when you get the right people in the right seats, everything accelerates.

## Delegating Outcomes

This is the difference between "Can you post this?" and "You own the marketing results for the company." One is still yours. The other frees you to scale.

Delegating outcomes is one of the most powerful things you can do as a leader and one of the hardest. Especially if you've spent years doing everything yourself. The temptation to swoop in like I used to do, can be a hard habit to break. Or, feeling the pressure under the mental glass ceiling when you take back a delegation by saying I'll just do it myself "because it's faster." But the hard truth is that every time you do that, you're training your team *not* to lead. You show them that they can't succeed without your constant supervision.

That's micromanaging. And you no longer have time for that.

What actually works is team members taking ownership of outcomes. Inside my company, we call them End Results. Every team member owns a specific outcome, an actual deliverable or responsibility with clear metrics that we can all point to and say, "Yes, this was completed." This isn't a task of "follow up with an email" or "call the client back". Instead, they see it through until the result is met. This requires each team member to think critically in their role and expand into an intrapreneur.

But that starts with how I hand it off.

Before I delegate anything, I ask myself: What's the actual finish line here? What do I want them to *achieve*, not just do? I get really clear on what success looks like and paint a clear picture of the result. I share this vision with them upfront saying, "You're not just managing social media this quarter. You own the outcome: increased engagement, lead conversion, and a system that runs smoothly without my fingerprints." I also tell them how we'll know it's working, what specific metrics we'll track, what checkpoints we'll hit, and where they'll have full authority to make decisions.

And that's when a part of my job shifted from controlling to coaching. If you want your staff to act as intrapreneurs, you have to give them the freedom to do so, and that means they will make mistakes. Sometimes those are genuine mistakes, and often, they just won't do things the way you would. It's bound to happen and a key to how your team grows. The Executive Team and/or I can inspect anytime we need to, but you trust them to fail and figure things out on their own. When they need you, you'll be there to support, guide, and help them execute a plan.

## Bonus Delegating Outcomes

One of the clearest moments I've ever experienced about delegation didn't happen in a boardroom. It happened during a birthday lunch. Amy was sitting next to me, eating a falafel salad, when she suddenly started panicking. She was choking. I could tell she was still breathing, but something wasn't right. She ran to the sink, trying to throw it up, and I followed, patting her back, and trying to help her, though honestly, I didn't know what I was doing. She needed the Heimlich. I froze for a second because I didn't know how to do the maneuver. Then I saw Angela walking toward us and said in a clear, strong voice, "Angela! Heimlich!" She stepped in without hesitation and saved Amy. Turns out it was her esophagus, not her windpipe, but that wasn't the point. I didn't need to be the one with all the answers. I just needed to delegate the outcome to the person who could deliver it.

# CHAPTER 14

# SURRENDER MONEY

## What's Your Why, Screw the Benchmarks, and The Big Money Chat

The lights were dim, and I could feel the energy of the crowd shifting as music pulsed through the ballroom like it always did. The big-wig speaker onstage that had been flown in for the event had the kind of energy you'd expect. Big smile, big presence, big story. And then came the line we all knew was coming.

*What's your why?*

The answer was always a secret I kept close. One I buried at masterminds and conferences. The question never changed and the pressure to answer "correctly" never did either. When it was my time to turn to the stranger sitting beside me and share my why, I smiled and said what I was supposed to say: "My family."

But that wasn't true. It had never been true. The worst part of this secret was that I thought there was something wrong with me for having it.

My family is the most important thing in my world. That was never in question. But they were never my why.

When I set out to build my business, my "why" was clear. Financial freedom. Not the kind of freedom you put on vision boards (even though I tried) but the rare kind that puts a buffer between you and a dependence on people, systems, approval, or expectations. A lot of people call this F-You Money. Call it what you want, but it's mighty important.

Financial freedom wasn't something I said out loud when expressing my "why." Not in those early days, at least. I felt the judgment (real or imagined) of choosing my vision. Saying my family wasn't the core reason I was working all these hours and making all these decisions felt almost... morally wrong. But that shame wasn't mine. It was a borrowed belief, and I needed to return that package back to where it belonged: a culture that praised sacrifice over sovereignty.

I wanted independence and security that no one could ever take from me. That may not be your why, but I can tell you this: if financial freedom isn't somewhere in your foundation, your business won't make it to 8 figures. And financial freedom is personal, specific and nuanced. You have to find what your unique number is. I've seen too many entrepreneurs skip this step and crash later.

If Hustle is the fire, the spark, Surrender is a controlled burn. Harmony is basking in the heat, roasting a marshmallow, and Legacy is inviting others into the warmth you've built. The structure you put in place now sets not only the temperature of the life you'll live next, but the impact you can have. Surrender is the season for structure, and it will most likely take *multiple* 90-day seasons to execute. But it begins here.

I was one of the few female financial advisors in my world in the late 90's and 2000s. I'm 5'11", blonde, and at the time, I was bodybuilding. The preconceived ideas most people had about me were, in my opinion, laughable. On harder days, I did find it hurtful, but I was usually able to pull myself out of the downward spiral by gently reminding myself that their opinions reveal more about who they are rather than who I am. Did I mention that I didn't get a fancy MBA or have an internship with a Fortune 500 company? Nope. I have my high school diploma, just barely an associate's degree, and a whole lot of drive.

While my peers and other advisors pulled back on spending to maximize profits, I was reinvesting. I remember thinking, *Why would I not reinvest profit to create future revenue? Why would I chase someone else's version of success when I was building my own?* I put money into marketing, my team, and into building the machine that would one day multiply wealth for others. It made my numbers look lean and I got side-eyed in meetings. I was so sick of having to explain myself again and again. They couldn't see what I was building, because it didn't match their benchmarks.

But I stayed the course. My mindset at that time was that I wanted to grow the company. I wouldn't take the salary increase and profits as much as my mentors and other advisors recommended. I was completely going against the standard I was told to follow.

My peer Jamie took the course that was advised, the one that was more in line with industry standards. But, I didn't need a private equity firm to look at my profits in the hopes of exiting quickly. I wanted to take those profits and build. Both ways, Jamie's and mine, were anchored in values we had to identify in Hustle and expand in

Surrender. Jamie wanted profitability to attract investors. I wanted reinvestment to create longevity. Neither was the "wrong" choice. They were "right" for him and me.

So, I doubled down on strategy, marketing, and structuring my dream team. Then, something incredible happened: our revenue doubled.

*This. Stuff. Works.*

The year people thought my business looked weak since the profits didn't reflect the internal shifts I was creating, the next year turned out to be one of our strongest. I was never trying to look good on someone else's spreadsheet. I was building a company that could hold my dreams.

And what you build with your money and system now, in the Surrender stage, will greatly alter the trajectory of your business, your life, and your Legacy.

When we start talking about your personal legacy, "The Big Money Chat" is imperative. If you were one of my private entrepreneur clients, I would sit you down and tell you the truth you need to hear, not what you wanna hear. This is the part of Surrender where the real financial foundation is built. It isn't flashy, and it likely feels flat. Most entrepreneurs I've worked with find this part of the process painfully boring, and I don't blame them.

But this is where boring becomes the new magic. If you can stay with it, what feels dull today becomes the foundation for everything that lasts.

It most likely feels boring because you're detoxing from the dopamine hits. I've had SOS, Shiny Object Syndrome, too. Maybe this is you. You chase the next idea or object and then wonder why your business always feels like it's in an out-of-control fire. I get it. But trust me, *structure* is the fix. And once it kicks in, everything changes.

Looking back, I wish I'd shouted my answer to the masterminds' favorite question, "What's your why?" with:

*Financial freedom isn't just about what you keep, it's about what you create.*

The structure you build in Surrender is what allows you to scale impact, not just income. Yes, it was really cool to be named one of the top Financial Advisors in the country. I was proud of that. I still am. But it pales in comparison to what I'm doing now.

I didn't realize when I attended what felt like almost every conference or mastermind under the sun that my unapologetic drive toward financial freedom would evolve into something bigger. I didn't know it would become a movement that has the potential to impact our economy, countless lives, and shift the culture of this world. I didn't know it would lead to a vision of helping 1,000 entrepreneurs scale to 8 figures, and along the way, each give $1 million to the causes they care about. But it did. And, if you did the quick mental math, that's $1 billion dollars into this economy for impact that moves beyond a spreadsheet.

That's a *why*.

This vision didn't arrive by an "Ah-ha!" moment while driving down the country roads in rural Oregon. It came slowly, one piece of the picture at a time as I rose through the Entrepreneurial Spiral™. Through reflection, reinvention, and rise. But the most significant way it came through was by saying "No" to the alluring benchmarks and constant feedback from the boys club telling me what I was doing was "wrong" while I was in the Surrender stage of my business.

Now, I'm helping move $1 billion into the economy for good.

$1 billion flowing from the hands of entrepreneurs who are scaling with integrity, generosity, and vision. $1 billion reaching nonprofits, communities, families, and futures. $1 billion stewarded by leaders who understand how to hold wealth, and use it.

Because, honestly, what else are we here for?

When you're in Hustle, the idea of giving generously can feel overwhelming. You're just trying to breathe above water. There's no structure in Hustle because that's the Hustle, folks. But in Surrender, that's when structure begins to form. And I'd be remiss if I didn't encourage you to start thinking about your Legacy now. Because what you build here is what you'll be remembered for. You won't hit financial freedom and suddenly feel ready to impact your community or teach your children about generosity. The muscle has to be developed now.

Even if it feels small or slow, it still matters. I promise. You might not be able to influence many people the way you imagine with your current financial situation, but you could impact just one life. And that still matters.

Never underestimate your power to make a difference.

As entrepreneurs, we have the power to create real impact. I love the idea that making money and making a difference don't have to be separate. In fact, when you align your business with purpose and people, profits become a natural result, not just the goal.

What a fantastic why.

# CHAPTER 15

# SURRENDER MONEY TOOLS

## The 2% Club

Whitney, one of my private entrepreneurial clients, should have been thrilled, turning cartwheels and high kicking in the street. After building her online coaching business as a single mom fresh off a divorce, she had gone over the $1 million in revenue mark, a huge success, and for those of you keeping track, she is now in the 2% Club. Only 2% of all female-founded businesses meet the benchmark of hitting 7 figures. And Whitney did it with her back against the wall, holding a newborn babe. But, Whitney felt, well, broke. All this work, blood, sweat, and poopy diapers had left her feeling frustrated and flat. While one reason was her mindset, the other was that she was paying herself less *after* she hit 7 figures than she was when she was at $400,000. She hadn't yet learned how to scale her success sustainably.

Of course, she felt broke! That makes complete sense when you're taking a salary cut while experiencing a significant revenue increase. But that feeling led her to question everything and believe the solution lay outside herself. She started doubting her own proven leadership, forgetting that she was the one who had grown this business, built the systems, and made the strategic decisions that got her to this level. Instead of trusting her track record, her mindset said, *I need to find a new coach, the flashy one with the incredible drive and social media content.* Surely they must have the missing piece. Surely they could fix what she suddenly felt she couldn't.

In the Hustle, there is no solid foundation, so you just throw everything at it. Whitney was trying that approach again; a classic recipe most founders have concocted, myself included. She mixed half-baked strategies and discipline with her unique sense of play and excitement, and got just enough of a taste of success to keep going, only to be left hungry, wondering when true fullness and genuine feeling of success would ever arrive.

This was a painful time during Whitney's Entrepreneurial Spiral™. What should have felt like a celebration was actually worse than a plateau—it felt like a false rise. I've seen this again and again: founders who earned more take-home pay at $400K than they did at $1 million because they have to build the structure to *support* that revenue. All of those elements—hiring new team members, tech subscriptions, unexpected 6-figure tax bills, outsourcing marketing, and upgraded office expenses—are why they feel like they are making less at $1 million than at $400K. I know, because I was one of them, but mine was a conscious choice. I chose to reinvest and build reserves. I chose to play the long game. You can too, as long as you're clear on what this business needs to give you, and what you're building it to become.

You've got to build the house you want to live in for your Legacy.

Whitney was still looking for things, people, or ideas outside of her rather than understanding the time value of money. She had to lean in and become familiar with the cost of capital. When you're scaling, as Whitney was, you can't afford to treat business cash like personal disposable income. Personal income can feel like "play money," and that quick-reward mindset often spills over into business—swiping the card for a luxury retreat the week after a launch—before the numbers are even reconciled.

You've got to run (and understand) your numbers. Cover your operating expenses. Set your profit margins. Then ask, *"What does this business need to produce in order to fund the life and impact I'm building?"*

For Whitney, that meant knowing exactly how many clients had to enroll at what price to meet her goal. After running her numbers, we realized she only needed fifty people in one of her programs. That's all. With Whitney's drive and natural ability to sell, fifty people felt like a cakewalk. That's the power of focus. That clarity changed everything and gave her direction for her 90-Day Seasons Planning.

Not only did she hit that goal, she blew past it. Too many entrepreneurs hit a big revenue month and spend the money before it's even settled in the account. Yup, I've done that, too. They launch, they make money, and celebrate by booking the trip to the British Virgin Islands for the whole family. Then, BAM! Reality hits at 35,000 feet on the flight home: *How the hell am I going to service and produce everything I just sold?* They just made a massive leap in their business, but failed to account for the real cost and time required to serve the clients, and fulfill their promise. The money's been pulled out of the business, and now there's nothing left to deliver what was sold. It's an "Oh shit" moment if ever there was one.

And you might be in the middle of it right now. The best advice I can give my private entrepreneurial clients, and you, as they scale to 8 figures is to think like the CEO *during* their massive upgrade instead of chasing the dopamine hit. When you treat business cash like personal cash to fill that deep need for external validation, you risk finding yourself at sea level when payroll is due or cash flow tightens, and most likely reaching for a credit card just to build a bridge back to where you started.

## LLC Tax Strategy

With a bigger business comes a bigger responsibility and opportunity with your money. In Hustle, most entrepreneurs start with a simple LLC but never revisit it. As you grow past $1 million in revenue, you can lose tens of thousands in taxes by not having the right structure and tax election. Now is the time, like today, to review your business structure (LLC, S-Corp, C-Corp).

I also recommend consulting a CPA or tax attorney* to confirm your current tax election is optimized for your entity.

*Note: This material is for educational purposes only and does not constitute legal advice; consult a qualified tax attorney for guidance specific to your circumstances.

## C-Suite Role

In the Surrender phase, you're becoming a true CEO. That means receiving consistent compensation, not random transfers or whatever is left over at the end of the month. True CEOs are compensated at market rate. That's the standard.

This is your checkpoint to make sure you've set a clear, reliable salary for yourself and a big, personalized sign to increase it, even if it feels scary. Especially if it feels scary.

When I stepped into my CEO role during this phase, I made the conscious decision to embrace that identity fully. For you, it may look different. The Hustle and Surrender audits are the places to revisit if you're toggling between different C-suite roles: CEO, COO, CFO, or otherwise. Your decision will be unique to your talents and what you truly enjoy doing.

But make no mistake: whichever role you choose, it comes with a raise. Period.

## Expanded Operating Plan

In Surrender, we move from the hustle of chaos and guesswork to clarity and calm. You need to see your numbers in one place and in real-time. Remember that basic operating plan in Hustle we started with? Now is the time to build on that foundation and create an expanded operating plan and financial dashboard. This tracks the same components of the basic and then adds an expansion, growth and scaling plan, along with cash on hand for operations and reserves. I would recommend using financial software like Quickbooks or another accounting software to automate much of this for you.

Let's say you run a service-based business and it is now making around $2 million in annual revenue. You want to clarify your numbers so you can plan with confidence, pay yourself well, and grow your business.

**Projected Revenue:**

(The income you can realistically expect from your business.)

**Total Expected Annual Revenue: $2,000,000 (monthly $166,667)**

**Recurring Monthly Expenses:**

(These are costs you know are coming each month)

Office rent & utilities: $4,500

Software/tools/subscriptions: $3,000

Marketing tools & platforms: $8,000

Contractor/team support: $20,000

Your salary: $15,000

Payroll (your employee's salaries): $30,000

Professional services (Consulting, CPA, legal, etc.): $4,500

Miscellaneous/operating buffer: $5,000

Total Monthly Expenses: $90,000

**Annual Total Expenses: $1,080,000**

**Estimated Profit:** (Your revenue minus expenses = profit)

Revenue: $2,000,000

Expenses: $1,080,000

**Estimated Net Profit: $920,000 (46%)**

An Expanded Operating Plan includes planned expenses for intentional growth over the next year. Take a look at the example below:

**Projected Growth Expenses:**

Hiring a new team member: $6,000/month

Increased ad spend for growing: $4,000/month

Business consulting & Fractional CFO: $3,500/month

Growth costs: $13,500/month or $162,000/year

**Total Expenses $1,080,000 (recurring) + $162,000 (growth) = $1,244,000/year**

<u>**With Growth Estimated Net Profit = $756,000 (38%)**</u>

Money is more than just numbers. It's not just revenue in and expenses out. It's energy, it's a resource, and ultimately, it's a tool to be used to create freedom, impact, and legacy. As I said before, you didn't go into business to go broke. Let's make sure you don't and create the plan, now.

This is the moment where your hustle and hard work shifts into wisdom. You've built something incredible, and now it's time to let your money start working for you. You're no longer just a business owner; you're an investor. An investor uses money from their business to create wealth.

During the Surrender phase, you have a chance to step back and look at your personal financial life, not just the business, and ensure you're building wealth both in and out of your business. It's time to start setting intentional financial goals beyond the day-to-day.

As freedom is a core value of entrepreneurs, in Surrender, you begin getting your time back, which unlocks the door to other freedoms. You need time to plan intentionally with your finances and be an investor. You also need time to develop relationships that matter most to you, and time to pursue your life's purpose.

To achieve financial freedom, you don't need to be completely financially independent. However, you do need to develop a plan to reach financial independence and take action. In the Surrender phase, this is the time to develop that financial plan.

Financial independence is a specific destination and different for each of us. It's the point where your assets and income generate enough to cover your needs without working, which for most might take a lifetime to achieve. Financial freedom, on the other hand, is a state of being. It's the feeling of ease, clarity, and alignment with the flow of money in your life now and how you manage it. Financial freedom can happen in an instant; it's yours the moment you decide to create a plan and take inspired action toward your financial goals.

You can experience financial freedom at any income level, as long as you're in harmony with your money and acting in alignment with your intention. Financial independence may take time. Financial freedom is available to you today.

# CHAPTER 16

## THE RIGHT SUPPORT IN SURRENDER

I wish I'd known these services existed sooner. I had no idea that a fractional HR partner could help develop and implement a people strategy for the business I was building or that a fractional CFO could act as both a financial guide and strategist to ensure consistent profitability. I didn't know that a business consultant and advisor could serve as a true thought partner, advocating for my future.

I have now experienced the benefit of each over time, but what transformed my trajectory was the long-term value these advisors provided. Their collective expertise became the foundation for the portfolio of companies I've built, each one designed to serve entrepreneurs in a holistic way. My companies now provide executive support and consulting services, and I've become the business strategist and master planner I wish I'd had a decade ago.

When my team and I consult with entrepreneurs scaling toward eight figures and beyond, we always start with clarity, understanding the current state of the business, where the founder needs support, and what their numbers are really saying. This involves working closely with the founder and their team as well as the bookkeeper and CPA.

From there, we step in as the financial and business strategist, filling the role of fractional executive support and guiding them through the systems, mindset, and strategy that increase enterprise value. My gift as a maximizer shines here. I help entrepreneurs build the very structure that allows them to fire themselves and rise to the next level.

Surrender means trusting others to help hold your financial picture. Once your company passes $1 million in revenue and begins its climb toward $10 million, it's time to expand your support team. In addition to your bookkeeper and CPA or tax strategist, consider adding the following professionals:

**Fractional CFO**

Think of this professional as your financial thought partner and financial strategist. They will help you:

- Oversee your bookkeeper and ensure it's done correctly
- Set up financial dashboards for you to monitor
- Analyze margins, pricing, and product profitability
- Create and manage a business operating plan, forecast growth, and cash flow
- Plan for scaling, investing, or exiting
- Annual Business Valuation

Why it matters: You don't just need bookkeeping, you need strategic financial expertise to understand the story your numbers are telling you. You need decision-making support rooted in knowing your numbers. A CFO helps you stop reacting and start making wise and informed financial decisions.

### Fractional HR Support Consultant

When your team starts growing, having a human resource system becomes important. This Surrender stuff may not come easily to you; managing people is typically not the strength of an entrepreneur. Think of this type of support as your sexy structure dial 911.

They will help you:

- Set up hiring processes, onboarding systems, and that sexy structure
- Create straightforward career paths, promotion tracks, and succession planning
- Build compensation plans that support retention and growth
- Ensure compliance with labor laws
- Create a healthy team culture

Why it matters: If you're the only one deciding who gets hired, randomly give out raises, or what roles are needed next, you'll bottleneck growth. Having an HR system frees you to lead, not manage every personnel decision.

### Financial Advisor and Coach

You need one who understands business owners. Your business is likely your biggest asset, but don't neglect your personal financial life and how that integrates with your business.

They will help you:

- Help you choose the right retirement plan for your business (see more below)
- Coordinate with your CPA and CFO on tax-efficient strategies
- Design a personal wealth plan that aligns with your goals
- Ensure business income is converting into long-term security

Why it matters: Over the long term, if all your wealth is tied up in your business, you're at risk. A great advisor understands that YOU and your business are the best investments you can make during the Hustle and Surrender phase, and they will also make sure you're also building personal freedom and options outside your business when the time is right.

### Retirement Planning

As business owners, no one else is putting money aside for your future. No one else is going to take care of your family if you don't. This part is on you. You must be disciplined to arrange it for yourself, and it can be exciting. When you begin using your income to build wealth for you and your family's future, it will feel incredible.

One powerful and simple way to begin investing is by setting up a retirement plan through your business. It allows you to save for your future and reduce taxes now. There are many options available, and they can be a game changer because they come with generous contribution limits.

Not all professionals are created equal. Their past experience is very important to the advice you will receive. You may not need all of these roles at once, and many times, the right team can support you across all of these areas within their offerings at this stage.

## Putting the Oxygen Mask on Others

The voicemail was sheer panic. Words were combined, thoughts were scrambled and my friend's pitch was so high in nature, I could barely make out phrases. I had heard a variation on this voicemail since

I first started helping entrepreneurs: they just got hit with the dreaded six-figure tax bill.

"Six figures! Julia, what the... ?"

"Congratulations, this happens to all successful entrepreneurs. You've made it! While it might feel like a rather rude wake-up call, it is a signal to slow down and create a strategy that is proactive rather than reactive." After about 10 minutes of conversation (and some very deep breaths on my friend's part), I was able to onboard her as a private entrepreneurial client to help structure her business to save her $75,000 in taxes. From one conversation. And that is not unique. It happens all the time.

I don't care if the door you walk through into generosity is painted fire-engine red and marked: *I only did this to save on my taxes.* It just doesn't matter. Not to me, and it shouldn't to you either.

Because here is what I know to be true: once you start giving, it's really, really, hard to stop. It's wired within us to help others. Look at your business—you have a product or service that is *helping* others. Yes, there is a monetary exchange attached, but when you boil your business down to its most basic structure, you are solving a problem for someone, i.e., helping them.

But when you give generously, that elixir of good feelings is amplified beyond the service or product that was your brainchild. This is an impact that hits differently and becomes, in the best ways, addictive.

I often hear (and always detest) the phrase, "I wanna give back. I wanna give back to my community." Giving back implies that there was something taken, that something is owed, or a debt incurred. Or worse, reciprocity. That there is a tit-for-tat relationship between a business owner and their community.

There is nothing I *have* to give to my community. I want to give because *I'm generous*. It's who *I am*, not an obligatory check I feel forced to write. It is deeply rooted in my values and when I give generously, it comes from within. I have the immense privilege of being someone who is resourced with money, and if you are reading this book and scaling your business, you are, too.

I can look at a person's tax returns and know within 10 seconds if someone is giving generously in their life. But I can also have a conversation with them and deduce the same data in about the same amount of time.

Giving generously looks different in each one of the four stages of your business life. In Hustle, it might be time. The 30-minute conversation you had with your next-door-neighbor's niece who is interested in becoming an entrepreneur—that counts. The $50 you gave with gusto to a forestry foundation because you love birding—that counts. Event sponsorship that helped with brand awareness—that also counts.

In Surrender, you're beginning to see the bigger picture, asking bigger questions, and seeing the bigger problems you can solve beyond just your business. And if the gateway to solving those bigger problems in our world just happens to be you taking advantage of a tax incentive, *great*!

I'm glad I can help. I just love being generous. It's all the rage. You should check it out if you haven't already.

## THE SURRENDER CHECKLIST

1.  **Surrender Mindset – In charge, not in control.**
    Building something that can grow without you.

2.  **You Fired Yourself – Congratulations!**
    You are no longer the bottleneck. You've identified where you're essential and where you're not.

3.  **Magic Wand 2.0 - Build the business you want.**
    Creating the map from values and vision.

4.  **Level Up (WOW Outcomes) Map the machine.**
    Structure, but make it sexy.

5.  **Your #2 – You're not the only one.**
    You've found (or are developing) your second-in-command. They hold real ownership, not just tasks.

6.  **Hiring – Right people, right seats.**
    You hire based on values and skill. No seat fillers here.

7.  **Delegating - Delegate outcomes, not tasks.**
    Your team doesn't need a to-do list. They need the finish line. You give it to them.

8.  **C-Suite Role – Elevating your role.**
    You're in the seat. You're making decisions. You're paying yourself like it.

9.  **Money Mindset – ROOTS over rush.**
    You've shifted from Hustle money to rooted wealth. Your financial decisions reflect long-term thinking.

10. **Expanded Operating Plan – Expanding the dream.**
    Revenue, expenses, future growth, and profit. It's all mapped with
    a one-year strategic plan.

11. **Tax Plan – The IRS doesn't surprise you.**
    You're no longer surprised at tax time. You have a smart, strategic
    plan designed by your financial team.

12. **Retirement Plan – You're building your future.**
    You've moved beyond short-term wins. You're creating a financial
    future that serves you and your legacy.

# PART THREE: HARMONY

## The Harmony Process

# CHAPTER 17

# THE SWEET SPOT, "PINCH ME!" ENERGY

It was a private concert with Brian Adams.

Brian. Fricking. Adams.

A personal teenage crush, on stage, singing *The Summer of '69* to a crowd that screamed, and sang along with fists pumping to the conference room ceiling. I was surrounded by my incredible team as I danced and jumped in the way that only my thirteen-year-old self remembered. But I could barely hear myself over the roar of the crowd, the euphoria of thousands (probably also remembering their younger years) singing in unison was sheer bliss. I thought it couldn't get any better until I saw Jennifer, my VP of People and Operations, jump the barricade, American Ninja Warrior-style and land on-stage next to the man himself, dancing, singing, and having the time of her life.

Folks, we made it. This is Harmony. This is the sweet spot you've been waiting for. And, sure, maybe your Harmony isn't your head of

HR twerking next to Bryan Adams, but it was mine, all mine. I turned to my #2, Jason, and the smile that lit his face was priceless.

A different version of me—the one who stayed too long in the Hustle, or the one who was "letting go" of everything but inside still tightly holding on, the Diet-Coke of Surrender—would have wanted to be center stage. I would have wanted to grab the spotlight, to prove to the world that I was the leader in control. But I no longer needed (or craved) the external validation of being the #1 leader of my company.

And I've got to tell you: the sidelines? After I hustled and finally let go? Whew. They are some pretty amazing seats. In fact, they're a "pinch me" experience I want you to live in and normalize. Because it is possible.

It is possible to scale to 8 figures, and what's even more incredible is that *scaling to 8 is easier than 7*. If the first two sections of the book felt heavy, I can understand. Those were hard times. We built something out of nothing. But if you've followed the advice and guidance from this book, you've also created something remarkable—a business that can grow without you.

Does that mean taking a vacation? Yup. The business will grow.

Taking six months off to help welcome your first grandchild? Absolutely. The business will grow.

Cutting back to three to five hours of work per week? I promise, it will grow.

This is your "easy button," and a major shift in mindset I want you to start understanding. Because if you were raised in the Hustle, if you've felt the emotions of releasing and surrendering your "baby" by hiring that #2 position, then it can be difficult to believe that building a bigger business is easy.

But you have to get used to *different*. If you're knocking on the door of Harmony, you've made the leap from "me" to "we." And here's the beautiful part: you'll never want to go back.

You begin to feel even more expansion and freedom. You look at your team and think, *I can't imagine doing this without them, nor do I want to.* You feel trust. You are supported. You feel momentum, not because you're grinding, but because you're aligned and have a team working with you.

In Harmony, you experience the magic of having others care about your business as much as you do because you've learned to train and hire your team as intrapreneurs.

That's not a pipe dream. It's culture. It's leadership. It's what happens when you build a business that gives your team purpose, ownership, and a seat at the table. And as their leader, Harmony also means recognizing and appreciating others' contributions without needing external validation.

While Harmony is one of the things I'm most proud of in my business life, I did struggle with it. Several of my clients did as well. The spiral doesn't stop just because you're seeing $3–4 million in revenue, can take a three-week trip to the BVIs, or decide to take up tango dancing.

If you're still in Hustle or Surrender thinking, *Umm… how hard is it to simply coast? I'd love to have your problems,* I've been there. If you've only known struggle, Harmony will feel unfamiliar. And if you're not ready for the unfamiliar, it will feel scary.

Marcus, a physical therapist and one of my private entrepreneurial clients who originally wanted to scale to $10 million and came to me in his Hustle stage. He walked through the stages, shattered the ceiling in the spiral, reached Harmony, and sold his business for $28 million—impressive. But when he saw the check, something precious inside him recoiled at the money. All his life, all he knew how to do was work in his physical therapy centers. This check signaled something to his identity that didn't sit right. So, what did he do? He went out and created more businesses. Of course he did. If you're reading this, this might be you, too. Some of the businesses were successful, others weren't. But, as a private entrepreneurial client, when we would touch base, my consistent refrain was, "Dude, just go on vacation! Go golfing. Spend time with your kids!" He would laugh and say, "That's a good idea, Julia... yeah." And, then he would take a long weekend to golf with his sons. But not too long.

My husband had a different experience when he hit Harmony, but he isn't the typical entrepreneur. He doesn't take calls on weekends or check his email past 5pm (well... usually 2pm) and his company averages $5-6 million per year. But what he does is something called NoWork November, and he means it. For the entire month of November, he doesn't work. These days, his "workday" looks more like a couple of hours in the office to touch base with his team, if that. His team calls him if he is needed, but it has freed him to do the fishing, hunting, and sports he enjoys. He has a process. He is not the process. And because of that, he enjoys life outside of work, which allows him to be the most amazing husband, present father, and exceptional friend to the people he loves most.

Harmony is when your business begins to feel different. Possibility starts to merge in every direction; limitless impact and quantum growth. You're no longer the engine driving everything forward. You're no longer the one holding it all together, or the sole operator holding the keys.

And that's the gift: space, time, and energy returned to you. Your world expands. Your business scales. And the people around you begin to rise into their roles, into their leadership, into their full potential, just as you have risen into yours.

That night with Bryan Adams, I wasn't the center of attention. I wasn't proving or pushing myself forward. I was fully present, surrounded by a team I love, watching my VP of People dance her heart out under the lights. That was my Harmony moment. Not because I'd made it, but because *we* did. I wasn't the star of the show anymore, and I didn't need to be.

I had become the kind of leader who makes room for others to shine. When you finally let go, you don't lose your power, you multiply it. Harmony comes when you step into your full potential by giving others the chance to step into theirs.

And whether your version looks like selling your business, building a new one, NoWork November, singing from the crowd with arms around your team, or an all-out twerk next to Bryan Fricking Adams, you'll know it when you feel it. And that's the sweet spot.

# CHAPTER 18

# THE HARMONY MINDSET

## In the Pocket

I'm an entrepreneur first, a business and financial advisor second, and a champagne lover third. I know for a fact I wouldn't have recognized, let alone articulated, that it's easier to scale to 8 figures than to 7, if I hadn't set out to help other financial advisors grow their businesses.

As only 1% of businesses will scale to 8 figures, most entrepreneurs and founders will experience what is known as the infamous "Valley of Death" when leaping from 7 to 8 figures[1]. I watched them struggle to pass this threshold of entrepreneurship in the same ways I had, and I'd think, *Oh, they're in it. And it's only going to get worse if they don't learn how to fire themselves.*

---

[1] North American Industry Classification System Association (NAICS): https://www.naics.com/business-lists/counts-by-company-size/?utm

When I taught the Fire Yourself Framework™ and guided them through the Entrepreneurial Spiral™ — the process I lay out in this book—there was always a moment. Sometimes it was quiet, knowing what was coming. Sometimes it was met with resistance and a touch of resentment. Other times, it was that instant spark of understanding.

Truth be told, most entrepreneurs didn't want to believe it at first. They had spent years doing everything themselves, pushing through the early stages, keeping every piece together. They believed they were in control. The ones making it all happen.

The truth will set you free, but first it will piss you off.

But once they truly understood the shift, that it's easier to scale to 8 than to 7, there was this momentum.

At the 6- to low 7-figure range, your business still runs on your energy. Every decision, every fire, and every deliverable still finds its way to you. There's no true freedom in that. No room to grow without burning yourself out. What got you to 7 will never take you to 8. In fact, it's already holding you back.

8 figures requires something else. Something better. You stop being the operator and start becoming the architect. You build it so the business runs without you.

Harmony is the result. It's proof that you have fired yourself. The systems are working. The team is leading. The vision is expanding. And you're no longer the one holding it all together.

There are four internal mindset shifts I've seen in every 8-figure CEO who makes it through the spiral and lands squarely in the pocket of Harmony.

- We before Me
- Learning to Endure

- Own Your Seat
- Held by What You Built

Up until now, Hustle and Surrender had only one business mindset to address. But, this is the elevated space that you are operating in; there's more stretch and mental work required. It's not more complicated, just different. And Harmony is all about getting used to different.

## We Before Me

We were seated around a long conference table at the hospital foundation board meeting, reviewing the final vote on funding a major project. I was serving as President, and the motion had just passed. The majority said yes, but a few members weren't fully on board. I paused. It didn't feel right to just say "motion passes" and move on. That moment showed me how far I had come from needing to get my way. I didn't want to lead by majority rule. I wanted alignment.

Earlier in my career, I served on nonprofit boards and participated in Rotary where I learned Robert's Rules of Order, a strict system designed to quickly move groups through decisions by majority vote. At the time, I didn't question it. But the deeper I got into building a company based on Harmony, the more I saw how that kind of structure can work against lasting alignment. It silences valuable insights and leaves team members behind.

When I had finally surrendered the need to control everything to feel important and believe I had all the answers as a leader, something different opened up. A new kind of leadership became possible.

We have a team principle we live by: *be concerned for alignment.* That means when a new initiative is put forth, ask: who else is affected by this?

Who needs to be involved or represented? Not everyone needs to be in the room, but every perspective should be considered.

This idea came to life when we launched *Inspired Wealth*, our financial coaching program. It was a completely new offering for our clients. I was excited about it, but I didn't just run with the idea. I brought it to our executive team because I wanted alignment. I wanted to be pressure-tested, but I also wanted them to see what I saw: the potential for a total home run.

As the founder, it's important to have a safe place to share big ideas, even before they're fully formed. Some will be great. Some will be duds. But if your executive team is trained to ask smart questions, speak straight, and stay curious, it creates a powerful decision-making environment.

In our company, we use three alignment categories:

1. Aligned for: fully bought in, excited, and ready to go all in.

2. Aligned with: see the value, trust the vision, and support you to lead it.

3. Committed against: believe the idea is not in the best interest of the business or team.

As the leader, I need a one or a two to move forward. If someone is a three, we keep talking. We stay in the conversation until alignment is reached. That's how we make decisions. It's slower, but it's safer. It builds trust, and it scales.

This is what it means to shift from "me" to "we." I don't need to have all the answers. I don't need to lead every decision. I've fired myself from the need to be right. I defer to the leaders in their zone of genius. I know I've hired people who are smarter than me in areas I've stepped out of.

Alignment within our team is one of the factors in how we scale, but it also helps us keep momentum without burnout. Which is one of the most powerful gifts of Harmony.

## Learning to Endure

I didn't know until years later that my team called me "The Hurricane" when I wasn't in the room. And honestly, I can't blame them. My personality matches what the Kolbe assessment calls a Quick Start: someone who initiates fast, thrives on possibility, and acts before they overthink.

As an entrepreneur, I saw potential everywhere. I'd walk into the office fired up about a new idea, talk through projections, vision, execution, and hand it off in a whirl, all before lunch. I didn't realize that when I was spewing high-speed inspiration from the center of the storm, I left my team to clean up the aftermath. They didn't know what to execute, what to pause, or what to ignore, so half-built projects piled up behind us like debris from a Category 3.

Looking back, that season taught me something essential. I didn't need to funnel every idea into my team. I needed a thought partner, someone I could share the idea with before it reached twelve people and burned five hours. But I didn't have that yet. So instead, I defaulted to the team, and earned the nickname honestly.

The energy of the business told me that something was off, I had hit a ceiling. This part of the spiral called for reflection. *What was I contributing to the environment that was either serving or destabilizing?* While I didn't hear the term "Hurricane," I knew that as a leader, I needed a new way to engage with my team. Eventually, the systems stabilized. The right people were in the right seats, supporting the work and our clients. The company began to function like a real business, not just a reaction machine. And that's when something unexpected happened.

*I got bored.*

Everything was working and nothing was on fire. I could feel the emotional tumbleweeds blow through my heart. Most entrepreneurs experience something similar when the internal hustle quiets down and chaos disappears. There was space in my day and it made me uncomfortable.

It didn't come from scarcity. It came from abundance. And that made it harder to recognize, and even harder to resist. That's the shadow side of Harmony. When you finally build the business that runs without you, and your nervous system just might tell you to blow it up. You start searching for something to tweak, rebuild, or create just to feel active, to feel that sense of worthiness. There's a reason why habits and addictions die hard and why endurance, mixed with discipline, becomes the real work.

You don't need a new idea. You need to protect the one that's working. You don't need another funnel. You need discernment.

This is the moment when your external business reflects your internal capacity, and your leadership becomes the lid.

As John C. Maxwell says, "Leadership ability is the lid that determines a person's level of effectiveness." If you want to increase your impact, raise your lid. That doesn't mean doing more. It means developing yourself with intention and restraint.

Harmony challenges you to maintain what you've built without breaking it. If you don't understand how to live in a state of having, you'll instinctively return to Hustle because chaos feels familiar and can be rather attractive when there are no fires to put out or build.

That's why this is the season to lead from your highest self.

- Prioritize restoration and creativity over urgency
- Deepen your zone of genius, not expand your responsibilities
- Let purpose drive your next move, not boredom
- Protect your team's clarity as fiercely as you protect your vision

Let the calm center you. And if the quiet makes you restless, add more play to your calendar. Go paddle boarding at sunrise. Book the cooking class in Tuscany. Spend a Thursday morning painting with your kids or dancing in your living room to the music that reminds you of who you are. Visit a new city with no agenda. Plan a weekend with friends where business isn't allowed at the table. Let joy take up space again.

But don't mess with the system that took your Hustle and Surrender years to create. Let it support you.

## Own Your Seat

We had a partnership with a bank that used to send us a steady stream of client referrals. Then one quarter, the referrals slowed down.

My brain went straight into problem-solving mode. I started drafting plans to hold a lunch-and-learn, ramp up communication, maybe even show up at their offices to stir things up.

But I stopped myself.

That relationship wasn't mine to manage anymore. Someone on my team had been stewarding it for years. By stepping in, I would've undermined the trust and consistency they had already built. What I needed to do was talk to my executive team, not the bank. Ask the right questions, support the strategy, and own my seat at the table.

If *Learning to Endure* is about resisting the urge to overbuild, *Own Your Seat* is about resisting the urge to over-function.

By now, if you've done the work of Surrender, you've hired or promoted your #2. It might be a President or a COO. At minimum, I hope you've fired yourself from handling operations. From my experience, that's not where founders thrive. We aren't wired for it. In fact, most entrepreneurs loathe managing. And when we hold on to it too long, we stunt the growth of our team.

Your role has changed.

And that means not inserting yourself where your presence could actually disempower. It means believing in the people you've hired to lead and giving them space to lead.

## Held by What You Built

When you are in Harmony, the systems work. The business hums. The team moves with clarity and care. You've built a structure strong enough to operate without you, and you give permission to do so. That permission reflects the final mindset. Because you can't let the business support you until you've chosen alignment over control, endured through the quiet, and stayed in your seat when you wanted to fix things. This isn't the beginning of Harmony. It's the outcome. And it holds you because you built it that way.

That's a job well done.

# CHAPTER 19

# HARMONY TOOLS

## Magic Wand: The Trilogy

Congratulations (again). You've fired yourself from the day-to-day. You've built a team that leads with clarity.

Now, the vision is no longer just yours. It belongs to the culture of your business. This is the moment to define how it feels to work here. Not just what gets done, but *how* it gets done.

No one likes to be micromanaged. You don't like it, and your team hates it. A thriving team culture fosters empowerment and leads with principles, not just policies. You don't need a manual for every possible situation, you need a principle-based culture that guides behavior and creates psychological safety.

A good workplace isn't about free snacks or Friday check-ins. It's about shared values, clear roles, and permission for people to rise. When my team had questions about this book's title, I told them the truth:

you're here because I fired myself. Every new hire exists because someone earned a promotion and fired themselves from their old role. That's what strong culture does. People grow, roles evolve, and accountability doesn't depend on me.

*"Firing yourself isn't just for you—it's for your team, too."*

If you can lead and set your culture to a temperature that reflects the above, this is where the intrapreuneurs will thrive. So, ask yourself: if you could wave a magic wand, what kind of culture would you want to hold your team together for the next ten years?

What does leadership look like when it's not just you?

What kind of internal experience would make your company the best place your team has ever worked?

# CHAPTER 20

# THE HARMONY VALUES

## I got kicked off the bus.

The mission was simple: draw the bus. Not an actual bus, of course, the metaphorical one of our business. The one that would take our team into the future. So the executive team and I gave my entire staff time. Weeks, not hours. This wasn't a whip-it-up-in-20-minutes kind of thing. We gave them a whole month to create their vision of what our business looked like as a bus, who was on it, where it was headed and most importantly, *how* we were going to get there.

I just *love* this kind of thing.

On the day of our quarterly team retreat, we gathered in the conference room for the big reveal. Each person stood up, explained what they had drawn, and walked us through their vision. About half of the staff had me in the driver's seat with my #2 usually riding shotgun. Everyone else was spread throughout the bus in meaningful ways: some near the front, some in the middle, some tucked in the back as quiet powerhouses.

But the other half of the drawings surprised me. In those, my #2 was driving, and I wasn't even in the bus. I was on the hood, or on the roof, or somewhere outside of it entirely. My initial reaction wasn't grace or curiosity; it was a stunned heartbreak because at that moment, I didn't see myself as the visionary leader of this incredible team. I saw myself as discarded.

I remember laughing with my team and enjoying the presentations, but my mind was spiraling fast as my eyes scanned the room. You know those moments where a thought grips so tightly into your brain that you can't see outside of it? Yeah. That was me.

*They don't need me.*

*I'm not doing enough.*

*I've already been fired from my own vision.*

It hit the deepest root of my not-good-enough wound. That place where I used to confuse being replaced with feeling irrelevant.

I really wish I could have experienced that day differently. I really, *really* wish I could have embraced the faith my team saw in me. I wasn't kicked off the bus; I had risen to a new level and had been there for quite some time. This wasn't new to me or my team, but a part of me, a part I thought had left the building, decided to slide into that conference room, kick up its feet and make itself comfy.

I was outside the bus because I had graduated from driving it. *I had literally fired myself from that role years earlier.* As the founder and CEO, I had cast the vision and could see further than anyone else because it was my dream and it was my job to chart the path that only I could see.

They didn't need me at the wheel anymore because they trusted the direction I had already set.

They were saying: *We're excited and know where we're going. Now let us help decide **how** we get there.*

The version of me writing this now sees it all differently. But this is the real life experience where the deep, engrained muscle memory of the Hustled entrepreneur forgets that she fired herself. That day in the conference room, I stayed silent and said nothing about what it triggered in me. Internally, I had spiraled downward. That's what fear, shame or living too long in the Hustle does. It distorts my view of myself and my talents. It turns my exceptional leadership skills against me into a version of loneliness that wasn't rooted in truth. That was the story I told myself.

But, I wasn't out of the picture, and I wasn't meant to be on the bus. I was supposed to be on a higher, better seat. That is the reward for the risk that I shouldered in those early years, but my mental glass ceiling came pressing me down, making my internal world small.

I had achieved many milestones at that point; a 7-figure business, Forbes recognizing my expertise, and I still felt like I couldn't sit at the cool kids table. But, I built that bus, and everyone had a seat on it. Mine was just at the top.

And that, really, is Harmony. I just couldn't hear it at the time.

My team supported me even when I was caught in the leftover of old Hustle patterns. That is what I had built, a business grounded in shared trust, vision, and strength. Together, we created something bigger than a bus. We created our culture.

We went from drawings on paper to values that define the soul of our team. These values weren't just theoretical or performative but reflected in our everyday decisions and how we treated one another.

Harmony isn't about just having the systems in place to grow. It's also about having the team create (with colored pencils and all) a plan for how we want to get there.

## Team Values & Culture

*You don't need twenty values. You just need a handful that mean everything.*

The best cultures don't just have values posted on the wall. They have values you can feel the moment you walk in: the laughter between co-workers over a shared memory, the way a difficult conversation builds trust instead of eroding it, the birthday celebrations complete with your choice of ice cream cake, cupcakes, or tiramisu.

Think of your rockstar staff members. The ones you wish you could clone and ask:

- What do our best team members consistently embody?
- What behavior do we reward, and what do we never tolerate?
- If I stepped away for six months, what would I want to see still thriving?

The culture of your business determines whether you have a business that fuels you, or drains you. This chapter is about creating a business that breathes with you.

When people feel safe, seen, and inspired, they give their best. They think for themselves. They innovate. They speak up and care. That's the energy needed at 7, 8, and 9 figures. Not just doers, but team members that are intrapreneurial, acting as players with ownership mindsets and behaviors.

Some examples from our business include:

- We do what we say we'll do
- We speak straight and listen generously
- We take 100% responsibility
- We acknowledge, appreciate, and celebrate each other
- We solve problems instead of creating drama
- We always seek alignment within the team
- We practice inclusion
- We are for each other. We always assume positive intent from others

In the early days, team culture is often unspoken. It's "how we do things around here." Everyone knew that "urgent" meant yesterday, "ASAP" means now, the real decisions happen in the meeting after the meeting, and bad news waits for the weekly status meeting. But it's not written anywhere. It's the secret language learned over time that is only spoken in that business. Some businesses are built on this silent code. But as your business matures, culture must become intentional. It's the thing that holds everything together when you're not in the room. It's what allows your vision to be carried forward by others who believe in it.

Culture has to live in your actions. My team and I meet once a week, a group of 23 people currently. In 30 minutes, we go through one of our values. That is our way.

What might you and your team want?

Here's how my team and I operationalize it:

## Weekly Team Meetings

Don't you hate it when a meeting could have been an email? Yeah, me too. In the wise words of Adam Grant, meetings need to do one of four things: decide, learn, bond, or do. Otherwise, it should be an email.

We keep our weekly team meetings simple with a clear purpose is to bond and learn. We acknowledge and appreciate team members (bond), we focus on one value of the week (learn), updates (learn) and then close by someone stating our vision or our commitment (bond). It's about 30 min every Wednesday morning but it keeps the momentum up with our team. We have 4 different locations and this time together is the imperative glue that holds our culture intact.

## Quarterly Team Retreats

These retreats hit all four metrics of bonding, learning, deciding and doing. Every quarter, my Executive team meets together for strategic planning, followed by a full team retreat day; we close our offices, fly out our virtual team members, and enjoy having some fun together while we map out our next 90 day Season together.

## Team-Based Hiring Process

An important principle in our company is *Be For Each Other*. From the first interview through every season of a team member's career, we are for them, not against them. That commitment begins during hiring. We vet candidates together to confirm they have the skills for the seat and share our values and working style.

Here's how it works:

- **Step 1: Initial Screen** – Jennifer, our VP of People & Operations, reviews candidates and has the first one-on-one conversation. This stage focuses more on character, values, and whether the fit is right for both sides rather than on skill sets.

- **Step 2: Small-Group Interview** – The candidate meets with their potential manager, Jennifer, and a senior leader over Zoom. Not only do team members have permission to voice their opinion if they sense misalignment, they are expected to.

- **Step 3: Assessments** – Candidates complete role-specific and values-based assessments that measure both capability and alignment.

- **Step 4: Team Interview** – The final interview takes place at the nearest office with 8–10 team members, while I join via Zoom. This is our double-triple-absolutely-yes moment. The team watches how the candidate interacts in a group setting and weighs in on cultural fit. I depend on my team to catch what I sometimes miss, because I tend to see the best in people.

Only after all four stages do we extend an offer letter and employment agreement. The process can take thirty days or more, but it ensures alignment, trust, and buy-in across the team. A resume shows skills; our process shows who someone really is.

## Onboarding

I would rather run a marathon in heels than onboard a new employee. My patchwork SOP was, "Can you just follow me around?

Hopefully you'll get it." Folks, this is a shameless reminder for you to, once again, fire yourself from the things you hate doing.

Most turnover happens in the first six months, which makes sense when you think about how chaotic onboarding usually is. Fast-growing companies rarely take time to build a real process, and I was no exception. Treating someone like a shadow or tossing them into the deep end with a "I hope they swim" mentality doesn't build loyalty or culture. It causes confusion, and eventually, they'll leave.

Enter Jennifer, again.

She turned onboarding into a strength for our culture. Day One for a new hire now means a goodie basket on their desk, a virtual welcome card signed by the entire team, and a catered lunch with their new colleagues. There is a detailed two-week agenda that guides them through each department, including one-on-one time with me. They can learn the business from every angle.

But where we truly shine is in our Culture Book. This isn't a policy manual; it's how we turn our values into practices. Each team member has a dedicated page with their favorite drinks, go-to snacks, hobbies, families, and even their fur babies. We include inside jokes and, most importantly, how each person likes to be recognized. Not everyone wants the same spotlight when they crush a milestone or go above and beyond for a client, and the book honors that individuality. It's as playful as it is personal, a tangible reminder that we value the whole person, not just the role they fill. For every new hire, it's like being given a starter kit for connection. They can quickly see who we are, understand how we connect, and why they, the new hire, belong. That sense of belonging turns day one into the beginning of a long, meaningful journey with us.

## Handbooks & SOPs

If onboarding is the welcome mat, handbooks and standard operation procedures (SOPs) are the structural integrity of the house. I used to dread handbooks and SOPs as much as onboarding: boring and stifling. As entrepreneurs, freedom calls to us every day. But as I've grown, I've realized these best practices give me peace of mind, and that peace is the freedom I seek while leading an 8-figure business.

Unspoken expectations are simply poor communication from leadership and foster an eggshell culture. That's not interesting to me. Being clear with my team is being kind to my team. They deserve to know exactly what is expected of them, how we treat each other, how we serve our clients, and how the work gets done.

I despise rework, errors, and wasted time on things that could have been streamlined. Documenting how we do what we do doesn't create a box, it creates structure. And, as noted earlier, structure is sexy. Clear standards and consistent practices don't just protect the business; they lay the foundation for every team member to flourish, including me.

## Career Tracks and Team Development

Big companies have endless ladders; smaller companies like mine must show new hires the opportunities from the start. I understood this in theory, but when my VP of People, Jennifer, stepped in with the initiative and intrapreneurial spirit she's known for, the impact was dramatic. Our team turn-over rate decreased, recruitment success skyrocketed, and employee satisfaction boomed.

Career tracks address the question of the "how far can I go here" problem and make the future obvious when a team member joins. In my financial services company, a client service associate can see the financial advisor path, step by step, and understand the outcomes they need to achieve as they advance in rank. This kind of clarity attracts intraprenuers, keeps A-players, and helps expand every aspect of the business, including me. A newcomer can arrive with little experience and still build a full career here, because the path is visible and the progress is earned.

## Founder Energy

As the founder, your energy *influences* the culture. If you're burned out, stressed, or resentful, your team will feel it and the culture will be impacted because of where you are energetically. You can assemble the best team, implement the best practices, and keep the machine running smoothly, but if you are still trying to control everything, nothing will function properly. Culture starts with your decision to fire yourself from doing it all.

## Team Culture Checklist

Use this to assess where your culture stands. If most of your answers are "no", take a 90-day Season to focus on turning these questions to "yes."

- Do we have clearly stated company and team values?
- Does each team member understand their role and the definition of success?
- Do we have weekly team meetings for alignment and accountability?
- Are we holding quarterly events and strategic planning sessions?
- Does our hiring process evaluate for values and energy fit?

- Are we promoting from within and providing clear career advancement paths?
- Do we celebrate successes and establish rituals for recognition?
- Do we foster a culture of safe and honest feedback?
- Are our team members committed and thriving?
- Do we make time for fun as a team?

# CHAPTER 21

# HARMONY AUDIT

I was sitting across from Ray Scalfani—my business coach, turned mentor, turned friend, depending on which one of us you ask—at one of my favorite restaurants in Dallas. I fly out there once a quarter to get myself into the kind mental pretzel that comes from loving personal development. It makes you stretch, question your own blind spots, and strip away whatever ego still thinks it's in control.

That day, Ray said something so clear it made me stop mid-sip: *If you grow without scale, it's chaos. And if you scale without growth, it's bankruptcy.*

Well, there it was.

That one sentence summed up a decade of trial and error, and it was exactly what I needed to hear now that I was transitioning between Surrender into Harmony.

Let's get clear on the difference and what I learned from Ray. Growth is about more; more clients, more revenue. Scaling is about increasing your operations and structure; it involves investing in hiring, creating systems, and technology. Growth without scaling creates bottlenecks. Scaling without growth bleeds cash. But when both are aligned? That's the business mic drop.

Folks, that's Harmony.

Growth can feel exciting but without systems, it becomes chaotic. Think: more clients, more revenue, but also more stress, more team to manage, and without order, that can create excess drama, and ultimately, less time for you. Growth is driven by effort. On the flip side, scaling is intentional. It means building structures that allow your business to grow exponentially while reducing your personal workload. Scale feels strategic and smooth and is powered by people and systems.

You need both. Growth drives momentum. Scale sustains it. But they have to work together and at the right time.

So, pause here, and check in with where you are.

Ask yourself:

- Can the business operate without me for a day, a week, or a month?
- Are my margins shrinking, even though revenue continues to grow?
- Is my team overwhelmed, with no room to breathe or think?
- Am I working harder than ever but not seeing better results?

If you're nodding along, it's time to scale. And scaling requires clarity, strategy, and support.

This next part of the book will guide you step-by-step on how to shift from growth to scale, and why creating harmony in your business isn't just possible. It's essential.

## Growth Phase: The YES Years

This is where most entrepreneurs start:

"Yes, I'll take the project." "Yes, I'll figure it out." "Yes, I'll do it myself."

This is beautiful. It builds resilience and our experiences. But at some point growth for growth's sake, without a plan, is a recipe for burnout and chaos. You've made it past the Hustle stage and have the structure that is sexy, but you can't keep operations running like this forever.

You might recognize this by your internal mantra, "It's fine, I'll just do it."

Then you're likely in growth, not scale.

## Scaling Phase: The Strategic Shift

Scaling is about building something bigger than your limits and pushing the boundaries of your business. It requires you to think about costs that serve and a return on your time. You develop a repeatable process and let the business run it. Scaling is about making yourself irrelevant in delivery while staying essential to the vision.

During Hustle and Surrender, I was all in on increasing revenue and helping people. Profitability didn't get the attention it deserved. Then we hit Harmony, and whoops! We fully plateaued. And no, the spiral never ends. I had to step back and ask why everything suddenly felt so chaotic.

We took on too many unprofitable clients just for the sake of helping. My heart had entered the chat. I wanted to serve everyone, not just the wealthy. For years, business coaches told me to raise our standards and set minimum client requirements. *I hated that advice.* It felt like selling out. My team and I were proud of not having minimums. That was our war cry. But eventually, chaos took over from my heart-led initiative. My team was overwhelmed, turnover increased, and client concerns piled up. My team wanted to hire more help, but I knew that wasn't the answer.

We had a bigger problem on our hands, and since numbers never lie, I went looking for the truth, our truth, of the cost to serve our clients. One clear financial lens helped us pinpoint where things were breaking. We calculated our cost to serve by dividing total business expenses by the number of households served. That gave us a baseline for what it actually cost to support each client.

For example, if our total expenses are $3,000,000 and we serve 1,500 households, then it costs us $2,000 to break even on just one. If we're only bringing in $1,500 from that client, we're losing money. We're essentially paying them to do business with us. That's when the full picture clicked. I had spent so much time in Hustle and Surrender focused on growth that I had ignored profitability, and this was the result. We were operating with a model that couldn't support scale. If we didn't make a change, we would stall or face something worse.

So we made a change. But we did it in alignment with our values. I've always believed in helping people build wealth, not just serving those who already have it. We didn't want to slap on a high minimum asset requirement that excluded the very people we felt called to serve. Instead, we shifted our process to require a minimum revenue level. You want to work with us? Great. Here's the program, and here's the cost. That small pivot gave us the ability to say yes with integrity. Yes, we can help you. But this is what our services cost. That simple shift allowed us to stay profitable while giving potential clients the power to decide whether they valued what we offer.

What happened next was fascinating. The right people found us. Clients who respected our process, valued the work, and wanted to grow with us came in strong. The ones who weren't attracted to that offer fell away organically. We stopped being all things to all people. This change didn't just attract the right clients; it sent a clear message to my team that we value them, too. A true mark of Harmony. Profitability ensures we can keep our promises to our people, to our clients, and to ourselves. Ideal clients bring out the best in your team.

Was it difficult to pivot? *Absolutely*. But it was imperative. Sometimes, the spiral presents moments that are black and white and require a different version of you to fulfill your vision.

But if you're not watching all your numbers, and if you're not making these decisions intentionally, you're not really scaling. You're stalling in the plateau and need to reflect. Real scale happens when your process is solid, your systems are sharp, and your margins are clear.

## The Bonus Shift

As I moved through my Entrepreneurial Spiral™ and uncovered the true cost to serve, something else came into view: people don't doubt a process. They buy one. Your process is your intellectual property. It's your unique way of delivering value. Clients trust a proven process, and that's exactly what attracted the right people to us when we changed our offering. Our people and systems are what brings that process to life with consistency, every time.

When you scale, your process becomes a product. It becomes teachable, documentable, repeatable, and sellable. Because in the end, clients aren't buying your time. They're investing in the transformation you can lead them through. And they will pay a premium for a process that delivers it.

## Your 8-Figure Future WOW Outcomes Chart™ - Sexy Structure Gets an Upgrade

It's time to draw a new map of your growing future business. This is the power of structuring your business on one piece of paper. Every year we strategize and develop new roles for our growing team and then update our WOW Outcomes Chart™.

### FUTURE WOW OUTCOMES CHART ™
#### (Who-Owns-What)

**FOUNDER**
- Visionary Leader
- Creative - Idea Generator
- Big Problem Solver

**PERSONAL ASSISTANT**
- Care and feeding of founder
- Scheduling
- Calendar/Email management
- Administrative tasks

**#2 IN COMMAND (#1 IN CONTROL)**
- Manage the business
- People leader
- Culture keeper

**SALES LEAD**
- Drive revenue growth
- Manage sales & Ad strategy
- Manage business development

**MARKETING LEAD**
- Events, social media, email marketing & Ad creative
- Brand & Partnership management
- YouTube & Podcast management

**OPERATIONS LEAD**
- Employee/contractor mgmt
- Lead Freedom Dashboard™
- Client service & Processes
- Systems & Technology
- Workflow management

**FINANCE LEAD**
- Manage financials & Data analysis
- Forecasts/operating plan
- Strategic business support
- Oversee bookkeeping & Accounting

**BUSINESS DEV SPECIALIST**
- Business development support
- Track and nurture leads

**SOCIAL MEDIA COORDINATOR**
- Manage social media & Video production
- Website admin
- Marketing calendar

**OPERATIONS ASSISTANT**
- Implement process & Procedure
- Client relations assistance
- Email & Calendar management

**FINANCE ASSISTANT**
- Complete expense & Account processes
- Accounting
- Bookkeeping

If you want to clearly see the road ahead and identify who you need to hire to bring this structure to its full potential, create a Vision-Aligned WOW Outcomes Chart™ — a future-proof plan for your team. This

"Chart of the Future" lays out the vision for your scalable team and we're increasing your visibility as a leader.

In Surrender, you step back, but you don't go blind. For my private entrepreneurial clients, we build their own, unique Freedom Dashboard™ that tracks the leading and lagging numbers, so you'll either get confirmation it's working, or a check-engine light early enough to act. You need to monitor both leading and lagging indicators to make sure that your team members are owning the outcomes in the WOW Outcomes Chart™ and you see, rather quickly, who and what is working and what is not.

## What This Looks Like in Real Life

Every Monday, unless I'm traveling, I meet with my executive team to review the numbers and our 90-day focus initiatives. When I'm on the road, my leaders run the meeting. If I miss it, a five-minute scan of the Freedom Dashboard™ tells me exactly what's happening. We surface issues and opportunities fast, course-correct, solve problems, and celebrate what's working. The liberating part is knowing that if something needs a flag, the team raises it. This isn't about auto-generated reports clogging the inbox; it's about tracking the right metrics; clear, actionable, and used to make timely decisions.

The Freedom Dashboard™ for leading and lagging metrics should include:

**Lagging (rearview):**
- Monthly revenue
- Client retention
- Sales conversion rate

**Leading (dashboard):**

- Discovery appointments booked (this week)
- Sales team activity (appointments set)
- New prospects from marketing channels added (this week)
- Client engagement (meetings attended / touches)

Review the dashboard weekly with your executive team. Patterns emerge. Trends become clear. And with this clarity, comes power to pivot and adjust as needed.

This is working on your business , not in it. You will not only develop as the leader, but will grow and scale your empire. It might feel tedious, but it's the necessary step to owning a clean, growing, and scalable business.

In Harmony, the shift is this: *you can take the pulse of the business without stepping back into management.*

# CHAPTER 22

# HARMONY MONEY

## Pay Day

You've built the machine, let it run.

In Harmony, your revenue is growing, and profit is more predictable. Huzzah! All of those late nights, all of that ambition, that drive. It. Paid. Off.

As you fired yourself, your role shifted and elevated. You may no longer have time or desire to be the one providing the service or selling the product to clients. You might be spending more of your time running the business and working with your executive team. It's time to evaluate your salary and give yourself a raise that reflects the scale of the company you're leading. You didn't build a multi-million-dollar business just to underpay yourself.

Have your fractional executive support compare your current compensation against others running businesses in your revenue range. I find we are rarely our best advocates with salary and money. You're not holding a minor job. You're holding the vision and leading a growing company, managing the mental load of running the business, and creating livelihoods for your team. That should be reflected in your pay.

When your salary reflects your role and responsibilities, it reinforces your worth, grounds your leadership, and brings powerful energetic alignment for your business. Don't delay this. You've earned it.

And it's not just your time to cash in. It's time to retain the talent you have by making strategic investments in their future. Your fractional executive support team will need to benchmark salaries to ensure your team is supported and aligned with the market.

Here's how this looks:

- Continue working with your Fractional CFO to provide up-to-date business financials. Take the time to have them add in expansion plans and costs, cash flow forecasts, and review regularly with your executive team.

- Develop an operating plan with current-year and five-year projections, including a staffing plan. Make that financial forecast visible so leaders can take ownership.

- Allocate a spending plan to each department head for management and input, and enable other executives to view the financial flow, oversee sections of the operating plan, and take ownership of their responsibilities.

- Create a benefits package people don't want to leave, and implement a long-term incentive plan that keeps your top talent invested in the company's future.

## Clarity of Numbers

Clarity about your numbers. Clarity about your offers and services. Clarity about your team structure and roles. This is the moment when you stop flying blind and start making data-driven, intentional decisions. It's time to clean up your business so it can hold the next level of revenue, team, and impact.

Analyze your numbers. They always tell a story. And depending on how well you understand them, you'll see a story of profitability and growth or one of stress and scarcity.

Recently, a private entrepreneurial client launched a one-day intensive where five clients flew in to spend the day with her. Each paid $5,000, bringing in $25,000 of total revenue. Her expenses were an Airbnb for two nights at $2,000 and food for $1,000. That left her with a gross profit margin of more than 80%. That's an excellent margin and a sweet story of efficiency and clarity.

When she compared it to a five-day program, the story shifted for the worse. The price point stayed about the same, but the expenses increased significantly. Her margin sank below 80%, revealing a weaker model. Another private entrepreneurial client had a similar wake-up call. On the surface, her mastermind looked wildly successful. However, once she factored in heavy overhead and financing for participants, her profit margin was closer to 20 percent. The plot twist behind her constant stress became quite clear when she looked at her storyline of numbers.

As discussed, numbers tell the story of your business. The ones that matter most are:

- What is your true profit margin? For example, if you earn $25,000 in revenue and spend $3,000 on expenses, your margin is 88%.

- What is your ideal profit margin? If you carry debt or have high financing costs, you might need a higher margin to stay profitable.

- Which offer is your most profitable? Compare each service or product side by side to see which one consistently yields the strongest margin.

- Are you losing money on any offers? A low-margin or negative-margin product may need to be redesigned or eliminated.

- What is your cost to serve each client or customer? Add up your total operating expenses and divide by the number of clients. If you spend $1.5 million annually and serve 500 clients, your cost to serve is $3,000 per client.

- What is your annual revenue per team member? In my company, it is about $300–400,000 per person. If revenue grows by $600–800,000 in a year, that means we can confidently add two new hires.

- What is your client retention rate? A service-based business with a 99% retention rate tells a story of loyalty and sustainability. And that's one story I am proud to tell about my business.

These numbers aren't meant to shame you if you don't already know them. They are simply data, and data provides clarity. It reveals the next best action and provides the blueprint for what to optimize, simplify, and scale.

The practice is simple. Set your goals for each metric, track them consistently, and review them weekly on your Freedom Dashboard™. This confirms the accuracy of your business and makes sure the story your numbers tell is the one you want to be telling.

Let your numbers speak and let them tell a story worth shouting from the rooftops.

# CHAPTER 23

# THE RIGHT SUPPORT IN HARMONY

If you didn't hire fractional executive support help during the Surrender phase (most likely because you like to do all the things) this is something to do now. Until you are at $10 million+ in annual revenue it doesn't make sense to hire a full time CFO or CHRO.

At this stage, beyond $3M in annual revenue, you need a financial team that doesn't just keep score, but helps you drive strategic decisions. You're no longer looking at the past; you're planning the future.

Here's who you need on your financial dream team now:

### Strategic Bookkeeper or Controller – Forward-Focused and Detail-Oriented

This role is an upgrade from basic bookkeeping. You need someone who can help manage financial workflows, ensure timely data, and partner with your team for better insights. They can provide:

- Accurate monthly closing with timely reports

- Management of accounts payable and receivable systems
- Job costing or departmental reporting, if applicable
- Support for internal controls and fraud prevention
- Cash flow monitoring and forecasting inputs

Why it matters: You need accurate, up-to-date data to make strategic decisions quickly. Sloppy books create delays, and at this level, delays cost real money.

### CPA Tax Strategist – Proactive and Integrated

Your taxes are more complex now. You need more than just someone who files your returns, you need someone who builds your tax strategy in line with your business and personal goals. They should:

- Create a custom proactive tax strategy based on your goals
- Align business income with your personal wealth strategies
- Coordinate with your financial advisor and CFO
- Make sure you're optimizing entity structure, benefits, and deductions
- Be available, at minimum, for quarterly check-ins

Why it matters: One wrong move can cost you six figures or more. At this level, strategy isn't optional, it's essential.

### Fractional CFO – Your Strategic Financial Partner

You've outgrown just looking at reports. You need someone who sees the full financial landscape, helps you set goals, develop forecasts, and understand how to fund your growth plans and scaling vision. They can provide the following:

- Build forecasts and operating plans aligned with your vision
- Identify financial constraints and help solve them
- Track key metrics and advise on pricing, offers and profitability
- Support capital raise or debt financing
- Help you think like an investor, not just an operator
- Help plan and facilitate an exit or private equity partnership

Why it matters: This is the point where you start moving from a 7-figure business to an 8-figure company. A great CFO helps you build a business of value and is always looking out for things you don't see coming.

**Financial Advisor for Entrepreneurs**

You're now earning real profit meaning it's time to think about how to grow wealth beyond the business and give generously. A Financial Advisor with experience in entrepreneurship can help you:

- Choose the right retirement plan from your business
- Build a plan to diversify out of the business and toward financial independence
- Align investment strategy with business cash needs
- Explore charitable giving, estate planning, and legacy

Why it matters: Your business may be your biggest asset, but it shouldn't be your only one.

You're building something significant and lasting. That means it's time to surround yourself with experts who elevate your thinking, challenge you strategically, and help you protect the wealth you're creating.

Ask questions. Don't be afraid to say, "I don't understand." The right team won't just support you, your business, they will help you expand it.

## Giving Plan

In Harmony, you get your time back, finally! You no longer invest only money; you invest presence. This was the season I began serving on boards, donating to small art communities on the Oregon Coast and supporting our rural health programs. Those causes were personal. After my daughter's accident, I experienced firsthand the depth of gratitude that comes from receiving exceptional care in a rural community. The charities and organizations I chose reflected not only my values but the most formative, and at times painful, chapters of my life.

All the seeds I planted early on in my Hustle stage, and at times when I believed the ground would never give life, finally came. Now, I've launched my $1Billion for Good initiative driven by the belief that people with wealth can create profound waves of change when they lead with service and generosity.

## THE HARMONY CHECKLIST

1. **Harmony Mindset – 8 figures is easier than 7.**
   You're building smarter, with your team, systems, and alignment. You've found the sweet spot.

2. **We Before Me – Let your team lead.**
   Alignment with your team.

3. **Own Your Seat – Stay in your lane.**
   You do what only you can do and trust your team to do the rest.

4. **Learning to Endure – Stay in the pocket.**
   When success feels stable, boredom or sabotage can creep in. Harmony requires you to resist the urge to burn it all down.

5. **Team Values – Speak the same language.**
   You've named and operationalized your company's values. Your culture now leads through shared principles that do not require your presence.

6. **Team Culture – Build a business that breathes with you.**
   You've created a values-driven culture with empowered intrapreneurs, not just employees. They take ownership, bring ideas, and move the vision forward.

7. **Growth vs. Scale – Know the difference.**
   Your business no longer expands at your expense.

8. **Sexy Structure – Design the machine. Build your 8- or 9-figure future.**
   Your WOW Outcomes Chart™ is clear. Roles are defined. Departments have owners. Everyone knows the vision and how they contribute to it.

9.  **Strategic Expanded Operating Plan – Anchor to action.**
    You have an expanded operating plan aligned to your vision and a plan to get there.

10. **Weekly Tracking – Freedom Dashboard™ tells it all.**
    You track the data that matters. Every week, you and your team review key metrics that move the needle.

11. **Money Mindset – Pay Day: Give yourself a raise.**
    Yes, another one.

12. **Money Mindset – Know Your Numbers: Profit with precision.**
    Create the foundation by gaining clarity with your numbers.

# PART FOUR: LEGACY

## The Legacy Process

# CHAPTER 24

# MOM, YOU'RE FAMOUS!

"Oh my gosh, Mom. You're like... famous!?!" My middle child, Jasmine, looked at me with wide-eyed incredulity dancing in her 17-year-old eyes. A mix of awe, wonder, and a little bit of shock embedded her blue-green eyes as the realization hit: her Momma was famous, at least in this room. "Everyone knows you," she continued as she looked around at the mass of powerhouse female financial advisors gathered in the San Diego ballroom for my broker-dealer's annual conference. I had just come off-stage from speaking and leading a panel of other female financial advisors. Her gaze roamed across the room and then finally landed back on me, as if she had finally solved a 10-year puzzle, "And everyone wants to know what you think."

It was at that moment, perhaps for the first time, that Jasmine saw me differently. I wasn't just her mom, but an entrepreneur, a leader, and a whole person outside of the role of "Jasmine's Mom." I was someone who had their own dreams, desires, and ambitions.

LET'S GET YOU FIRED

Several months later, when Jasmine applied to colleges, she shared with me her personal essay to accompany her full application. In it, she wrote, "When my mom walked on stage at the conference, in her pink suit with dazzling rhinestones on the sleeves, I felt empowered to see her doing what she loves, and to say, 'That's my Mom.' Being at this conference, seeing my mom in her power, leading with her whole heart, changed something in me. I saw a path that was always right in front of me, and now I'm excited to walk my own way. I have always known that being a female business owner is the path that I would take, but being able to see a woman, who just happened to be my Mom, stand in her success and help other people gave me the permission to do the same for my career, my life."

This was, of course, the same child who wanted to be a client so she could schedule time with me. The fear that once left me terrified about my future resurfaced when I was caring for my daughter, Katelyn, a time when she needed my full presence, love, and attention. I worried that by being a mom, I might lose my career. I feared I would lose a vital part of who I was: an ambitious woman set on impacting people's lives for the better.

When I saw Jasmine's college message, it clicked. All along I was building what my mentor, Ray Scalfani calls, "a Living Legacy." Legacy isn't just what you leave behind; it's the paths you reveal to others who need direction. It is the modeling you show to those who haven't seen someone who looks like them in positions of power. And it's what you give this world, with the time that you have, that transcends money.

# CHAPTER 25

## LEGACY MINDSET

### Begin with the End

"I've written my eulogy every year since I was seventeen, Julia."

The island breeze whipped Britnie Turner's long brown hair into a frenzy, but she stood as firm as the ground beneath her feet on Buck Island, now known as The Aerial BVI, the stretch of earth she purchased at the ripe ol' age of twenty-six. The audacity and brilliance of this woman were undeniable. I first learned she had bought the island and in doing so became the first documented solo female to purchase an island in the British Virgin Islands. Yeah, she is in the not-so-secret club of BVI island owners that includes Richard Branson, but Britnie's story stands apart.

And while the accumulated wealth is impressive, it was her ability to keep her own ending close that struck me most. "I've always been aware of my mortality, our mortality," she said, opening her arms as if to include all of humanity. "No one and nothing has taught me more than that one exercise."

I thought about Katelyn's near-death experience when she was so young, and my middle child, Jasmine, who is now 17-years-old, imagining them composing their eulogies. The thought was sobering. And life-altering.

It might be tempting to dismiss this as a perspective that comes easily to someone crowned Miss North Carolina and who later became an island owner. But Britnie was also practicing that ritual when she was living in her car for nine months, unpaid, teaching herself real estate by rehabbing derelict properties. Her rise was transformative because her vision and faith were transformative. But for Britnie, wealth was never the goal: "Wealth is just a tool, and that tool needs to be in the hands of the right people."

Three years later after living out of her car, she became the first woman to own an island outright in the BVIs. That island is more than a symbol of triumph; it is a haven for healing. Britnie had already cut her teeth on the hard work of rebuilding abandoned, needle-strewn apartments and flipping blighted properties in Nashville while launching her real estate development company. When she later stood on Buck Island in the aftermath of two record-breaking hurricanes, she recognized a similar need on a global scale. From that experience grew Aerial Recovery (see giving resources to learn more), her nonprofit that takes the tactical grit veterans once used in combat and applies it to humanitarian missions. Where unskilled volunteers faltered, Britnie saw a gap she could fill. Today, former Green Berets and first responders deploy to the front lines of hurricanes and human trafficking hot spots, bringing their "boots on the ground" expertise. The same precision and courage once used on the battlefield now rebuild homes, restore communities, and rescue lives.

The path Britnie took is not for everyone; to live in your car, work for free, fighting to move forward when others doubt you. But it was Britnie's, and it's become part of her legacy.

So, what's yours?

You weren't just born to build wealth. While this book will help you do that, you were also born to create something meaningful, something that will outlast you. Death and taxes are certain, but what you do in between shapes the legacy you leave.

If you were to write your eulogy right now, what would it say?

Think about it.

How does this eulogy make you feel? Is there a shift in your perspective on your life? Do you have any regrets? Did you tap into something new or unexpected? Maybe a hidden desire?

These aren't conversations or thoughts that come easily. This isn't small talk at a fancy cocktail party or fleeting thoughts when stopped at a red light about where you want to vacation. This is the purpose of your soul.

Totally casual. Simple stuff, right?

But when you allow yourself to think deeply about why you're here, it transcends anything your business on its own could ever achieve. Because your business can be more than profit or growth; it can carry your values forward, influence lives beyond your own, and leave an indelible mark that outlasts your time here.

# CHAPTER 26

# LEGACY TOOLS

## Magic Wand - The Ripple Effect

This is about more than an exit strategy. This is about the stories people will tell because you chose to lead with purpose. It's about building something that outlasts you and the impact you will have.

If you could fast-forward ten, twenty, thirty years from now and see the impact of your living leadership, what would be different because you were here? Who would it reach? What would it leave behind?

This is where you start shaping the part of the story that will keep going, even when you're not in the room.

I've used these series of questions and thought experiments to help expand upon the values that I created way back in Hustle. The best tool I can give my private entrepreneurial clients who are entering or are in Legacy is a question: What do I want to pass on that money never could?

The grind of Hustle, the release valve of Surrender and the sweet spot of Harmony all play a part as you might contemplate the limitations that money can offer this world. At this stage, we start to wonder, "What else can I do?" The first question, posed in the previous paragraph is the North Star that directs all of my actions. But to dig deeper, the following questions can sharpen your steps.

### 1. What will my generosity teach others about what's possible?

My generosity can show others what's achievable. Not just checks, choices. Saying yes to bold bets, mentoring the next founder, opening doors that used to stay shut to others without my current resources. Money sparks the ripple; modeled behavior keeps it going.

Now it's your turn to answer:

_____

_____

_____

_____

_____

_____

### 2. How do I have to live now, so that I never have to question if I left a Legacy for good?

Legacy isn't just for later. I live it openly, in the present, teaching my kids how to be responsible adults with kindness and compassion, showing them what a healthy partnership looks like with their dad, doing what I love in helping entrepreneurs, keeping my promises, building margins for giving, making time to mentor, and choosing a long-term path over quick wins. It's in the way I live, love big, and lead.

That way, I never have to wonder if I've left a legacy for good, I'm actively practicing it.

Now it's your turn to answer:

_____

_____

_____

_____

_____

_____

### 3. How do I want people to feel because they were impacted by me?

I want those I meet to feel seen, trusted, and capable, not rescued. I want those I meet and help to feel activated and inspired. They leave with dignity and tools, not dependence. That feeling lasts longer than any gift.

Now it's your turn to answer:

_____

_____

_____

_____

_____

_____

### 4. What do I want to be remembered for?

In my professional life, I don't want to be remembered by titles, headlines, or even my name on a building, but by developing and encouraging people, by creating new, innovative ways and building businesses that continue to serve long after I'm gone. A clear playbook for impact, leaders who give because they saw it done, and ripples that reach farther than I can see.

Now it's your turn to answer:

_____

_____

_____

_____

_____

_____

## $1B for Good

I didn't set out to lead a movement. I started with one goal when I was 23 years old: financial freedom. I wanted to build a business that gave me options, created security for my family, and gave me time back. That was the dream. And it was enough, until it wasn't.

Over time and as I spiraled into becoming the woman I wanted to be, a much grander vision formed. I began to see what was possible if more entrepreneurs scaled with intention. What could happen if success wasn't just about more, but about meaning.

My vision now, and we touched on this in Surrender, is simple: help 1,000 entrepreneurs build 8-figure businesses and commit to giving away $1 million each as they do it. That's $1 billion poured back into the world. For good.

Imagine what $1 billion could fund: suicide prevention, mental health support, food security programs, clean water, financial literacy, business incubators, educational scholarships, regenerative agriculture, shelters and support services for women and children escaping abuse, and the kind of deep local work that changes lives generation after generation.

Entrepreneurs have that power. We are builders, innovators, problem-solvers. We are wired weird, and thank God we are! Because that means we can also use our ambition, know-how, and desire to change this world for the better. When we align our businesses with a higher purpose, we create value that goes far beyond revenue. We lead in a way that changes culture.

I'm not just helping your business scale. I am scaling impact, and I would love for you to join me.

Legacy doesn't begin when you sell the business. It begins the moment you decide to build something that matters.

So what do you want to give while you build?

Not to prove yourself or out of obligation. But because you can. Because you are wired that way.

If you are scaling and building, this is the time to start giving generously. It doesn't matter if you are in Hustle, Surrender, Harmony, or Legacy.

**Take the pledge. Build for good. And lead with love.**

Visit my website at https://www.thejuliacarlson.com/give
or scan the QR code below.

## Finding Your Fingerprint

Legacy is like a fingerprint of your values. It leaves a mark, and no two are the same. Britnie Turner bought an island in the British Virgin Islands and turned it into a sanctuary for healing and restoration. I've committed to investing a billion dollars into the economy for good by helping entrepreneurs scale and give generously. And my mentor-turned-coach-turned-friend, Ray, shows us another way.

I first met Ray when I was still building my firm. His coaching shaped some of the most important decisions I made as a leader. He's the one who told me, "If you grow without scale, it's chaos. If you scale without growth, it's bankruptcy." That insight changed everything for me. What began as a coach to coachee relationship evolved into a full-blown mentorship, and now into a peer pipeline where we continue to sharpen each other's thinking. Somewhere along the way, that invested time turned into friendship.

Ray is living into his twenty years of legacy. He calls it his 20•20•20 plan.

The first twenty were for stability: a corporate climb built on discipline, relationships, and saving enough to one day leap. The next twenty were for entrepreneurship: founding Clientwise, a firm built on the belief that great advising starts with great humanity. Even the logo carries a lesson; the dots over the i's connect from small to large, light to dark, then begin again, forming a circle of trust that signals the beginner's mind and partnership. It's a visual reminder to meet each client where they are, imagine the next future together, and then start again.

Lastly, his next twenty (and I imagine throughout the rest of his life) are for philanthropy and living his legacy. Ray refuses to treat legacy like an obituary word. For him, it's not what's written after you're gone but what you calendar while you're here: the local board seat, the hour spent mentoring a kid who needs a steady adult more than a speech. It is the choice to invest time first, bring your unique talent second, and write checks third, not because money matters less, but because money lands better when time and talent have already prepared the ground.

He still keeps a photo on his desk of the dented 1977 Corolla he drove through college, no A/C, parking backward on hills so he could pop the clutch. That photo is a compass, a quiet reminder of how far intention can carry you. His connection to his past self, and to others climbing similar hills, is what creates his living legacy and keeps him grounded.

I love the rhythm of his framework. Our legacies sound different, but they rhyme. Mine measures in entrepreneurs who build wealth and give it forward; Ray's unfolds in twenty-year seasons of purpose. Together they remind me there's no single way to leave a mark. Legacy might be an island that heals, a business that fuels generosity, or a life lived in disciplined twenty-year movements of purpose.

What matters is that you choose it with intention, and start now.

# CHAPTER 27

# LEGACY VALUES & LEGACY AUDIT

## What Breaks Your Heart?

Start there.

There may be many things. But what's the one that stops you cold every time? The thing you can't unsee. That's where you begin to form and curate the values that belong to your Legacy. Start with what is meaningful to you. That's how giving becomes personal and packs a whole lot of power.

The values you've named throughout this book have shaped who you are, how your business serves its clients, and how your team operates as a whole. They've built your culture and sustained your growth. But here, at the Legacy stage, those values take on a different currency. They stop being just the principles you operate from and become the imprint you leave behind.

What will be left when you are no longer in the room?

It's not always comfortable to ask. Especially if you're still navigating the fog of Surrender. When you're making payroll by the skin of your teeth, global impact can feel like a fantasy. But don't overlook what's already in motion. Legacy doesn't begin when everything's dialed in. It begins when you choose to lead with intention, even in the middle of firing yourself.

If you're not sure where to start, return to that first question: What breaks your heart?

And then return to your eulogy: What story do I want my life to tell, not just in business, but in how I gave, mentored, modeled, and loved?

That's where your Legacy begins, and a new story can start.

To help you name it, walk through these moments:

**1: The Close-Up – the moment.**
Picture the instant your chest tightens; the news story, the hallway conversation, the quiet detail ingrained in your brain. Stay there for a breath. *Which value gets louder like a never-ending earworm?* Name it.

_____

_____

_____

_____

**2: The Table – the company you keep.**
See the faces you'd invite when this comes up: one teammate, one peer or friend, one partner you trust. Hear the sentence you'd say out loud, without apology. *What do you care enough to say in front of them?*

_____

_____

_____

_____

### 3: The Tuesday – life at normal speed.

Imagine a plain ol' Tuesday twelve months from now. You haven't "arrived." You're still building. *What looks different because you kept caring?* A conversation you're having, a door you opened, a practice you honored. This isn't fanfare, just evidence.

_____

_____

_____

_____

### 4: The Echo – the story others tell.

Lean out ten years. Someone you helped is talking about you to a friend. *What single line do you hope they borrow?* Let it be simple, human, and true.

_____

_____

_____

_____

# CHAPTER 28

# LEGACY MONEY

## How much is enough?

How much is enough? That's the question at the center of Legacy. While you used the prompt, "What breaks your heart?" to find your purpose in giving generously, and "What do you want to pass on that money never could?" to align with your values, this one is money-based. And the answer won't be the same year to year or even season to season.

Early in your career, enough might have meant paying the bills and building a cushion. Then it became about flexibility, choices, and freedom. But somewhere along the spiral, enough becomes something else. It becomes *impact*.

The quote I return to often is this: *To have and not to give is often worse than to steal.*[2] That one stops me. Because it reminds me that accumulation without contribution isn't freedom, it's fear in disguise.

Most entrepreneurs are building toward financial independence. That's good and necessary. But once your needs are met, your questions must evolve. Now it becomes: *What will I do with what I've built? Where can it make a difference?*

Legacy mindsets are moving targets. They change as you grow. One day, it's building schools. Next, it's helping a neighbor through a quiet crisis. It might shift again when your kids head to college, when you become a grandparent, or when a conversation with a stranger pulls your heart toward a cause you never saw coming.

That's the beauty of this stage: it invites curiosity. Abundance isn't static. It expands when you stay open.

In the Legacy stage of your business, you have a target you are moving toward; your "enough." The number will be different for everyone, but the heart of it is the same: financial independence. At some point, the work is no longer about survival or even comfort. It becomes about securing your life and directing your wealth with purpose.

Enough might look like selling your business for $20 million, paying taxes, and living beautifully on the remaining $15 million. It might look like keeping the company but stepping back into a founder's role, working one or two days a week because you love it. For some, enough is mentoring the next generation, serving on boards, or guiding leaders

---

[2] Ebner-Eschenbach, Marie von. *Aphorismen*. Berlin: Franz Ebhardt, 1880 (revised ed. Berlin, 1893). "Haben und nichts geben, ist in manchen Fällen schlechter als stehlen." (Tr. Annis Lee Wister: "To have and not to give is often worse than to steal.") Note: exact page number not determined.

who will take the vision further. For others, it's a portfolio that funds both family freedom and meaningful giving for generations to come.

Whatever form it takes, "enough" is the point where your business becomes more than an income stream. It becomes a platform for impact, a foundation for Legacy, and a way to keep writing your story long after the day-to-day is no longer yours.

That is where money becomes Legacy.

# CHAPTER 29

# THE RIGHT SUPPORT IN LEGACY

By the time you reach Legacy, chances are you've built your dream support team. You have trusted advisors in tax, finance, and HR, and your CPA, financial advisor, and executive support are all in place. But here's the question most entrepreneurs overlook: *Who is holding the full picture with you?*

You've outgrown the stage of tactical advice. What you need now is a strategic advisor who can see the entire ecosystem of your business and your life—someone who can lead master planning that aligns your company, your personal financial goals, and the impact you want to make. An advisor who can think critically, see around corners, and ask the deeper questions that move you from success to Legacy. Someone who can help you exit with purpose, not just profits.

The truth is sobering: only 20–30% of businesses that go to market actually sell, and nearly 80% of an owner's personal net worth is tied up in their business. Even more concerning, 83% of businesses have no written exit plan. That's why the right guidance at this stage is non-negotiable. Below are the essential elements, your must-haves, to ensure that your Legacy is protected, your wealth is transferable, and your impact you've envisioned for years will truly endure long after you've fired yourself.

## Exit Strategy

Every business owner should have an exit plan. The *Fire Yourself Framework*™ and *Entrepreneurial Spiral*™ are the frameworks needed to set yourself up for a successful exit. Even if you have no plans to sell, you still need what I call a "Hit By The Bus" plan. It's not fun to think about but life happens. Exit planning isn't just about walking away; it's about leading your business into its next chapter with intention. As an exit planner and advisor, I help my private entrepreneurial clients prepare for this long before they're ready to sell. We focus on maximizing business value, strengthening leadership through the executive team, and creating options.

There are two primary ways business owners exit: internal succession or external sale (through a third-party sale, acquisition, or IPO). Exit planning is best done at least three to five years before your ideal exit, longer if your business is complex or deeply tied to your personal leadership (which is exactly why you need to fire yourself!). Be patient and intentional; you don't want to be in a rush. The goal is not just to protect an asset for caution's sake, but to preserve the lives it impacts: your loved ones, your team, and your clients.

Everything you've built through my *Fire Yourself Framework*™— moving from Hustle to Harmony—naturally increases profitability, freedom, and enterprise value. Done right, exit planning unites your goals, wealth, and legacy so your impact continues long after you step away.

## Business Valuation

Get your business valued every year. It doesn't have to be a major expense, an informal valuation provides a quick, affordable way to check your yearly benchmarks and track progress. We offer this kind of informal business valuation for our private entrepreneurial clients annually. However, If you're preparing to sell, that's when a formal valuation becomes essential. It's a deeper, more detailed (and more costly) process that's part of your exit strategy.

Both valuations are important, but for very different reasons. The informal keeps you aligned with your goals, while the formal helps you capture full market value when it's time to exit. Staying current on what your business is worth gives you incredible insight to ensure you're on track to hit your "enough number."

## Tax Optimization

You don't know what you don't know and this is where most entrepreneurs lose hundreds of thousands of dollars without realizing it because they have outgrown their CPA. Are you structured for maximum tax efficiency and long-term value as your net worth is growing to 8 figures and beyond?

## Personal Estate Plan

Legacy planning is more than just having a will and trust; it's a strategy for how your assets live on. Diversify your business and real estate holdings, align your investments with long-term goals, and ensure your estate plan reflects the life and impact you want to protect. With the right advisors, your wealth can continue to grow and serve long after you are gone.

## Charitable Giving

Your giving should flow from what you value most. For me, that has meant supporting the arts, rescue missions, helping those in need, and rural health care since Katelyn's accident. For you, it may be education, the environment, or local community needs. Partner with experts who can help you structure your giving so it creates the greatest impact while preserving your vision. Please see the resources section for additional information.

# CHAPTER 30

# WHAT DO I DO NOW?

People ask why I don't work one or two days a week like my husband does. I could. I've built the business to allow it. But I don't want to.

I'm still lit up by what we're building. I'm still chasing bigger questions, bigger service, a bigger vision. And I don't mean bigger for ego's sake. I mean *deeper*. More intentional. More generous. I still have work to do.

The problems I was solving when I was 23 and fresh-faced as an entrepreneur are not the problems I need, or am meant to, solve now. I am well-resourced and have the privilege and pleasure of solving *different* problems. Not out of scarcity, but because this is the good stuff. This is the purpose work. Once you implement the tools in this book, once you let go and scale, you open up space, not just for yourself, but to give. Many of my clients move from success to significance, turning their achievements into meaningful contributions. They start foundations, lead impact-driven ventures, and become benefactors in their communities.

That's the kind of empire I've built and am continuing to build. One that's rooted in structure, powered by service, and fueled by curiosity. I have an insatiable hunger to keep learning, to keep growing, to keep making things better not just for me, but for everyone connected to what we've built.

Think back to a time when someone breathed belief into you; when their words sparked something in you that felt like life itself. Do you remember that moment?

For me, there was a time when I was unsure, unsteady, and questioning everything. I was 23 and had just started my company. But I had a champion. Someone who saw something greater than what I could see in myself. Maybe that's where I get it from, because Howard's impact on me, my life, and my legacy, was a lead domino to me now, 48 years old, writing this book.

Howard was the one who encouraged me to start my own business. He planted the seed, and when I started to grow, he stuck with me. He would be present with my new clients at our first meeting that he had referred to me. I was young, new to the business, but determined. And the clients could sense that. We all knew what Howard was doing in those meetings: he was showing maturity, mentorship, and giving the clients a sense of trust with their hard-earned money. Howard might have gotten me in the door, but my grit kept me in the room.

We are all here on a journey, and part of that journey is remembering we don't have to do it alone. The right people show up when we're willing to invite them in: mentors, partners, and teammates who believe in us before we fully believe in ourselves. Howard did that for me, and I've carried that lesson forward in every stage of building my business.

So my final encouragement to you is this: don't carry the weight by yourself. Surround yourself with the right people, the right structure, and the right vision, and let them amplify what you're here to create. That's how you keep building, not just a business, but an empire that lasts.

Now go, and live it.

# LET'S BUILD WHAT'S NEXT TOGETHER

You've built something extraordinary, now let's take it to the next level. Whether you're scaling from 7 to 8 figures, preparing for an eventual exit, need an advisor to look at your full picture, or simply ready to create more freedom in your business and life, my team and I would be delighted to partner with you.

We offer a no-obligation, one-hour strategy consultation to help you identify the next right steps, whether that means maximizing the value of your business, creating a clear exit roadmap, avoiding a six-figure tax bill, or taking the first steps toward firing yourself. Wherever you are in your journey, we'll help you get on the right path.

At my companies, we help founders like you design thriving, scalable companies using the Fire Yourself Framework™ from this book.

Schedule your complimentary strategy consultation at;
TheJuliaCarlson.com/workwithme

# GIVING GENEROUSLY RESOURCES

The stories of organizations I've highlighted in this book have both inspired and impacted me greatly. If you feel led to give, I invite you to learn more about the incredible non-profit organizations featured on my website and explore ways you can make a lasting impact with your time and money. If you have a favorite non-profit and want to add it to this list please reach out to me, I would love to hear about it.

Together, we're building the $1B for Good movement where entrepreneurs and leaders are not only committed to creating wealth but using it for good to change lives.

Take the pledge, join my community, and let your success become someone else's blessing.

To learn more please visit thejuliacarlson.com/give or scan the QR code below.

# ACKNOWLEDGMENTS

This has been such a fun book to write. I know this work will never get old because it's my purpose! Every word, every story, every lesson has been divinely guided, and I'm so very grateful to God for making my life's path so clear even when I couldn't see it at the time or questioned the rough patches along the way. My faith and love for God have been my foundation through it all. I am beyond blessed.

To my hubby, Chris Carlson, my love of thirty years, what a journey we've shared! From the chaos of startup life to the wild rhythm of Hustle, every up and down was worth it to get here. We made it, babe. And in so many ways, it feels like it's only just begun. I love building this life and these businesses with you. Thank you for your endless support, for being my "kitchen bitch," and for always knowing what I need before I even say it. I love you, forever and always.

To my kids, Katelyn, Jasmine, and Jake, you are my greatest joy. My deepest prayer is that you find a path that lights you up and that you walk it with people you love. Thank you for growing up alongside this dream, for your patience when I worked hard, and for the laughter and adventures when we played even harder. Those memories are my favorite. I love you more than words could ever express.

To Keira Brinton, CEO of JOA Publishing and host of *Writer's Island*, thank you for being a true trailblazer and for showing women what's possible. You saw my vision so clearly and helped me bring it to life. This book was literally born on *Writer's Island* TV Show (check it out on streaming platforms for the behind-the-scenes of my journey!). That week was sacred, birthing ideas that had lived inside me for years and bringing them onto paper in the most magical way.

To Natalee Bloom, my gifted collaborator and dear friend, thank you for seeing me, being a champion of my story, and my life's work. You took my inspired, channeled words and helped me shape them into something truly special. This book wouldn't be what it is without your brilliant mind and your immense talent in developing the manuscript into the masterpiece it is.

To Elizabeth Copley, thank you for your meticulous editing and for ensuring this book was ready for the world to see.

To my private entrepreneurial clients, you are my inspiration. You are the visionaries, the builders, the creatives, the changemakers. Helping you expand your impact, wealth, and freedom is one of the greatest honors of my life. Thank you for trusting me with your most intimate money stories, your fears, your dreams, and your purposes. Let's go make an impact in the world!

To Ray Sclafani and Britnie Turner, thank you for sharing your inspiring stories. I am in awe of your devotion to helping other entrepreneurs rise to your level of success and deeply grateful that our paths crossed. What an honor to witness the living legacies you're both creating.

To Howard, thank you for being a mentor throughout my career and for believing in me before I did. Look where that faith led! I love and appreciate you.

And to my incredible team across my businesses, thank you for going all in with me. You show up with heart, excellence, and deep care for our clients and our shared vision. I am better because of each and every one of you. Jason Harris, my #2, I appreciate you taking such great care and stewardship over our companies. Jessica Beasley and Jennifer Webster, thank you for your support and energy for this project and helping with our private entrepreneurial clients. I love working with you all every day. With deep gratitude, thank you.

# BOOK RESOURCES

All book resources can be found at <u>thejuliacarlson.com/books</u>
or scan the QR Code below.

# ABOUT THE AUTHOR

Julia Carlson is an internationally recognized 8-figure entrepreneur, wealth mentor, author, speaker, and founder of multiple companies. Noted by *Forbes* and *Barron's* as one of America's top financial leaders, she belongs to an elite group of founders who have successfully scaled beyond eight figures and built enterprises that thrive without their constant oversight.

Julia started her first company at twenty-three with nothing more than an associate's degree and a vision to create something that mattered. As one of the few women in a male-dominated industry, every obstacle became part of her playbook for growth.

"I used to think wealth was just about money," Julia says. "Now I know it's about freedom. Freedom to live on your terms, engage in meaningful work, and leave something that outlives you."

Over the next three decades, she built four successful companies spanning wealth management, tax services, real estate, and business consulting. Her approach blended disciplined strategy with heart-based leadership, a combination that not only created extraordinary financial success but also cultivated a legacy built on trust and empowerment. Along the path of her entrepreneurial journey, she uncovered the truth that drives her work today: *it's actually easier to scale to eight figures than stay stuck grinding at seven.*

That discovery became the foundation for her movement and book, *Let's Get You Fired*, a counterintuitive approach for entrepreneurs who desire true freedom in their business and personal lives. Julia teaches that the path to eight figures begins by "firing yourself" from the parts of your business that keep you trapped. It's about being in charge, not in control. That shift, a radical reframe to most entrepreneurs, is what breaks the mental glass ceilings that keeps so many stuck in the seven-figure slough.

Today, Julia is helping entrepreneurs with what she wished she had early in her career: the roadmap and mindset to scale with ease, vision, and play.

Her mission is audacious and clear: help 1,000 entrepreneurs scale to eight figures and, in the process, guide each of them to give one million dollars to a cause that matters to them. Together, that's one billion dollars for good and a massive economic ripple of impact and generosity. *$1B for Good* isn't just a goal; it's a movement that redefines wealth as a force for collective transformation. Julia invites every entrepreneur who scales with her to take the pledge and become part of this living legacy, simple proof that business success and social impact are the same currency when led with intention.

When she's not leading strategy sessions with one of her private entrepreneurial clients, overseeing her companies, or speaking to audiences, Julia can be found hiking along the Oregon coast with her husband and three kids or toasting life's milestones with a glass of champagne.

# CONNECT WITH JULIA

 www.thejuliacarlson.com

 www.youtube.com/@thejuliacarlson

 @thejuliacarlson

 facebook.com/thejuliacarlson

 www.linkedin.com/in/thejuliacarlson/

 julia@thejuliacarlson.com

## Disclaimer Notice

This book explores the challenges and strategies of entrepreneurship, leadership, and business growth. It is intended solely for educational and informational purposes. Every effort has been made to present accurate, current, and reliable information. No warranties of any kind, express or implied, are made. Readers acknowledge that the author is not providing legal, financial, investment, or tax advice.

The content of this book is based on the author's professional experience, client work, and research, as well as stories shared by entrepreneurs and business leaders. Some names and identifying details have been changed to protect the privacy of individuals and organizations where appropriate. Every effort has been made to present accurate, reliable, and complete information.

The author and publisher disclaim any liability for any loss, injury, or damages resulting from the use or misuse of the information, strategies, or recommendations contained in this book. Readers acknowledge that any decisions or actions taken based on the material presented are voluntary and made at their own discretion and risk.

Readers are strongly encouraged to seek advice from qualified professionals, including certified public accountants (CPAs), tax strategists, and licensed financial advisors, before making any financial, legal, or business decisions. The author is not acting as a tax advisor or attorney, and this book should not be used as a substitute for personalized professional guidance.

Results are not guaranteed, as individual outcomes will vary based on unique circumstances, effort, and business conditions.

www.ingramcontent.com/pod-product-compliance
Lightning Source LLC
Chambersburg PA
CBHW020446130626
46549CB00001B/315